The View from

MARY'S FARM

❧

ALSO BY EDIE CLARK

The Place He Made

Monadnock Tales

The View from
MARY'S FARM

by Edie Clark

POWERSBRIDGE PRESS
PETERBOROUGH, NEW HAMPSHIRE

With the exception of "The Slipshod Reality" and
"The Afterlife," all the essays in this collection
originally appeared in *Yankee* magazine.

Book design: Jill Shaffer

First Printing October 2005
Printed in the United States of America
10 9 8 7 6 5 4 3 2 1   paperback

Publisher's Cataloging in Publication Data
   Clark, Edie, 1948–
     The view from Mary's farm / Edie Clark
       p.   cm.
     ISBN 0-9719934-2-4
     1. Country life — New England — Essays.
   I. Title.
   630.2—dc22

Library of Congress Control Number 2005908622

Powersbridge Press
6 Powersbridge Road
Peterborough, New Hampshire 03458

Order information: www.edieclark.com

CONTENTS

Acknowledgments

THE SOLITARY NATURE of these essays belies the many people who have helped in the compilation of this book. I am deeply grateful to all my editors at *Yankee*, most especially, Mel Allen, whose suggestion it was that I write these columns in the first place and whose friendship over the years has spawned many other works and ideas. I acknowledge also the gentle guidance of Tim Clark, Jim Collins and Michael Carlton, all in rotation. I am indebted to the many talents of Jill Shaffer. To Jonathan Meath and to Henry James. I owe a great deal to Katrina Kenison and Steve Lewers. And thanks always to Jud Hale, who makes all things possible.

As well, I am grateful to my neighbors who paved the way for me to come here to Mary's farm in the first place, chief among them, Anne W. Howe, a good neighbor and friend. And I'm forever grateful for all those who came before me on this land, Benjamin Mason who, in 1762, cleared the land and built the house and barn just after the end of the French and Indian War; to the generations of Willards, who sustained it into the 1940s; and to Mary Walker who came here with her family in the 1940s and whose gardens I try to keep, though, many have gone by. I couldn't even imagine keeping all the gardens Mary had here. I don't know how she did it.

ॐ Introduction

IN 1997, ALONG WITH MY NEIGHBOR, Anne Howe, I bought this farm, high up on a ridge in southern New Hampshire. Neither of us knew each other at the time, save for a few brief meetings. Our purpose was to save this farm, exposed to wind and weather but also to the magnificent mountain to the south. With no other houses in sight and no lights of civilization visible at night, it is a rare place in this 21st century. Mary's farm had weathered many storms throughout its history, which began in 1762 and has since encountered all the usual natural hazards such as fierce snowstorms and withering drought, as well as the hazards of man, most especially the threat, in the 1980s, by the state of New Hampshire to build a major highway through its fields. Mary, along with many of her neighbors, safely shepherded the place through that time of danger but after she died, her house and the nearly 200 acres all around it went up for sale. The more than forty acres of fields here represent the largest open space in this town. Eyeing the full view of the mountain, developers were eager to snap up the farm and build houses in the fields.

Easy money. It was this threat that brought Anne and all the neighbors back together again. I was a neighbor, in that I owned one of the barns that used to belong to the farm. I had used the barn as a writing studio for more than ten years. And that's how Anne and I, virtual strangers, came to buy Mary's farm together.

As soon as we took possession, we split the estate in two, using the natural subdivision of the road that cuts through the property. This yielded to her the fields which she absorbed into her existing property and yielded to me the house, the barns, the smaller fields, and all the legends that came with these pre-revolutionary shelters. Anne then put all her fields into conservation, which protects the land from developers for all time, and I set to work on the house and barns. By then I was into my fiftieth year on this earth. I would learn that I did not have the same strength and energy I had at twenty-five. But I still had the ambition of that younger self, a sometimes discouraging partner in what became a total renovation of the old farmhouse and much reorganization of the barns and the land. I had clearly taken on more than I'd imagined.

The other partner in the process was the writing of these essays, most of which originally appeared on the last page of *Yankee* magazine. I have always believed in the power of writing to accompany any time of strife, which came quickly at the beginning of my time here. Or expression of joy or awe, which, for me, grew out of that initial strife.

The place, it seems, will forever be known around here as Mary's farm, for Mary kept the gardens so beautifully for so many years and she was a benevolent presence on the land. For Mary and for her family, it was a farm that included horses and cows, chickens and pigs. In the barns, I see their remnants, manure in the stalls, hay in the lofts. Though I dream of having animals here and that may happen one day, for now this is a farm without stock (with the exception of my dog, Mayday), which is an all-too-common fact of life on these old farms. A neighboring farmer hays the fields, which keeps them open. Other than that, it's silent up here.

In this post-agricultural age, living here in this wild place, I sometimes feel like a sentinel, here to guard the past and guide the future of its open land. Though the barns are empty, there is, more than ever, an abundance of wild animals. Aside from the deer, moose, and bear, bald eagles have returned and I occasionally spot them aloft. Wild turkeys strut around as if they had never been endangered. In the early mornings, loons, who also have returned after a long absence, call as they fly overhead, commuting between the two lakes on either side of the farm. Bobolinks nest in the hayfields. Coyotes howl through the afternoons and evenings. And several of us on this hill feel certain we have seen a wolf, even though local wildlife officials insist we could not have. We reason that coyotes returned, so wolves could too. Why not? It is a different world up here, calmer than it was in the time of farming, but nonetheless nourishing. My first year here was daunting and, at times, frightening. There were times when I questioned why I had come — especially since my coming here was more serendipitous than deliberate.

I came here to this farm of memories without knowing why, except that it was in need and the views of Mount Monadnock were magnificent. I felt a draw that did not make a whole lot of sense at the time. But the pull was strong enough to get me here. My blind luck, I call it now. My vision improves with each passing year.

Harrisville, New Hampshire

July 2005

The Farm

❧ *Love Story*

FOR YEARS BEFORE I moved to Mary's farm, I had loved this place, passing by on the road home, slowing to look. There was usually something going on: smoke coming out of the chimney; a tractor in the yard being worked on; Mary kneeling in her garden, tending the phlox. And, always, there was the mountain in one or another of its seasonal moods. To have moved here as I did was a little like falling in love with an old friend, someone you have known for years, someone you never thought of that way. But, all of a sudden, there you are: I never thought Mary's farm would become mine and to be here is like the best, most rewarding kind of love.

Mary's fields, almost all of which are on the other side of the road from the farmhouse, have been open since the early 19th century and, so far as I know, always farmed. Over the years, the various farmers who worked these fields must have enjoyed their work. Walk up into the fields and the mountain is smack in front of you, and the fields, separated by hedgerows, roll out on either side, like something in England.

A few years ago, in the early spring, I began to notice that the trees beside the road were getting a much needed trimming. A young man, whom I did not recognize, was busy with his chain saw, selectively cutting the trees that had grown thick. He was carefully removing the brush and then raking, so that the roadsides looked beautifully groomed, almost combed. I had rarely seen such care taken in work like this. In spots where it had been obscured by these trees, the mountain was now grandly present, which made my ride home all the more pleasant. In well chosen spots, he left certain white birches as accent.

This went on for a couple of months. One day, I spotted the young man at work beside the road. Instead of his chainsaw, he was working with carpenter's tools. The road that passes by Mary's house is cut into a bank, which makes entrance to the field a bit challenging. Into the steep bank, he was building a flight of wooden steps. The next time I came by, the steps were adorned with pots of flowers and in the field, there was a freestanding white arbor, which appeared to me like an illusion or mirage: there had never been anything in the field but hay. With the rising steps and the distant arbor, set as they were facing the mountain, this seemed like the entrance to paradise.

I looked forward to my ride home from work, hoping to catch the next act in this silent play. My next ride by, I was not disappointed: everywhere around the farm, there were flowers — in pots, in vases, in bundles tied with ribbons. Set in the field, facing the arbor, were neat rows of hay bales. Carefully laid on each bale was a white cloth. Pews! There was going to be a wedding — a most elegant outdoor wedding! I wondered who could be getting married. Mary was a widow in her seventies, and, as far as I knew, both of her daughters were married. Perhaps a niece or nephew?

I wasn't the only one who had been keeping track of this wedding-in-the-works. Several people in town drove up to the hill on that Saturday and watched from their cars as the couple joined together under the arch. Later, I heard the story, told often by a woman in town who calls this "the love story." A young man who knew Mary and loved her view, asked her if he could be married in her field. In return for the favor, he said, he would cut the trees beside the road and open up her view. For the bride, he would build steps up into the field.

The arch and the linen-covered hay bales are long gone but the tidy roadsides and the steps remain, to remind me of that spring of ardent preparation by a diligent young man. A wonderful love story and I am as surprised as anyone to discover that I am now enjoying the benefits, inside a love story all my own.

❧ *Crystal Nacht*

I REMEMBER THE SEVENTH of January of 1998 as if it were some momentous day, the birth of a son or the death of a parent. It was kind of gloomy, a misty, warmish day with a rain falling, gently. Three weeks before that, I had bought this new house, known to many as Mary's farm. I did not plan to move until my old house was sold and so the house at Mary's farm, which is about three miles away from where I had lived before, sat empty, waiting for me to fill it with new life.

Every morning I went over to Mary's farm to check on things. That morning the mist hung, still and heavy, like a curtain. I walked through the chill cloud to the back door and went inside. It was cold and forbidding in there. I made my rounds quickly.

Back outside, I could barely see my apple trees through the mist and only the trunk of the enormous sugar maple in front of the house was visible, the great top being obscured by the fog. I had loved these trees for years, driving by, admiring the gnarled, poetic reach of the branches of the apple trees and the huge, perfectly round head on the maple, which I judged to be probably as old as the house, parts of which date to 1762. At that moment, the mist obscured them from me but I felt their height and their protection.

I started off to meet the day. The rain was more like a mist, nothing, really, but an annoyance, a gray and dismal space to move through. But overnight, in the high elevations, the rain turned to ice. I got up early and went up to the new house. As I drove up the hill, which is about 500 feet in elevation above the house in Chesham, I could see the tree trunks gleaming in my headlights.

At the house, the driveway was sheer as a skating rink. I drove halfway in and parked. Planting my feet as squarely as I could, I stood up. Rain continued to fall, greasing the ice. Using a coffee can full of sand, I sprinkled a path for myself. A slight wind had come up, enough to move the branches, and there was a heavy clicking sound as the iced limbs tapped against each other. As I reached the door, I heard a shot. I turned toward the woods but saw nothing. Another shot rang out. And then another. The shots multiplied until I felt I was in the midst of a firing range.

I wanted to cover my ears and run. The sound of the forest breaking frightened me, not for my personal safety, for I stood at the edge of a hay field, but for the enormity of it. There was nothing I could do to stop what was happening. Moving on clenched feet, I hurried toward my car. All around me, ice fell from the branches with the startling sound of precious crystal falling onto hard cement.

The can of sand was empty and I slivered along on the sheer surface. In an effort to gain a foothold, I stabbed down onto the ice with the heel of my boot. Instead of penetrating the ice, my thrust served to propel me upward, like a cartoon character, launched on a banana peel. *Whoops!* Up I went and then, *crash!*, down onto my backside. In an embarrassed instant I was back on my feet, glad that the crystalized world all around me had no eyes.

I did not hear the crack but maybe that is because there were so many other things breaking at once. An x-ray later that week revealed a broken rib, which explained the pain, a huge ache near my heart.

It was months before my rib healed. I'll never see the scar. But the trees revealed their pain in abundant display. One of my apple trees split open like a flower, the big branches crashing onto two separate roofs. The biggest arm of the old maple in front of the house sank onto the old but rugged roof. The reality of it stung me: these ancient, beautiful trees, which perhaps took root before our nation did, gone in such a swift and silent attack.

Our roadsides remained a shambles for months afterward, dried brush mounded like dense thickets. At the edges of our fields, the snapped-off tops of our trees stabbed like swords into the thin air. And, everywhere were the gaping stumps of our big trees, reminding us of our crystal night and the deafening sound of our broken hearts.

ॐ *Balancing Act*

IT WAS WHEN HE WAS preparing to pull down the lean-to off the barn that Ethan suggested he might be able to help me jack the house. "I figure we could run the steel beam from the stone wall over to here," he said, stepping crosswise to the corner of the house. Some 240 years ago, Mary's farm had been built into the side of a hill so that the ground floor on one side was the second floor on the other. A stone retaining wall divided the levels. It was this ground floor that needed and would receive a new foundation. And in order to provide that, we were going to have to lift the house out of the way so that cement could be poured and stones laid.

I'd known Ethan over the years, but never very well. I'd heard he was a college professor, which was true. And then I heard he was a logger, which was equally true. Now he was offering to lift my house into the air. I felt that anyone who could teach and cut wood could probably do the third as well. We conversed deeply about the way in which the house would be lifted, raising the corner onto the beam and taking the rest of the house out from under it. Ethan went home to sharpen his pencil, as he put it, and give me a price on the job. By the next afternoon, we had struck a deal.

On the appointed day, Ethan arrived early in the morning with his equipment, a big excavator and a twenty-foot steel beam. In the back of his pickup he had a load of cribbing: short lengths of 6 × 6 beams that he would stack, log-cabin style, to hold up the beam while it would be busy holding up the house.

Ethan is a big man, with thinning red hair and pale blue eyes. He spoke precisely and demonstrated with his big, splintered hands as if he were giving a lecture. He clearly wanted me to understand what he was going to do, and most of all he wanted to relieve any worry I might have that my house, so recently purchased, might collapse before my eyes.

I can't say I hadn't reviewed that possibility. I was relieved, then, that I had to be at work while he worked his black magic. When I came home from work, half my house hung in midair. I stood back and looked at the precarious affair, which reminded me of houses on the West Coast that had been undercut by mudslides. Cars passing by on the road slowed nearly to a stop to view what probably looked like the site of a disaster. Ethan was finishing up, stashing chain and cable into the back of his truck.

"Is it all right to walk up there?" I asked.

"Well, sure," he said. "Just don't be having a dance up there tonight."

He left and I went upstairs and stepped gingerly into the bedroom, beneath which the beam labored like Atlas. I took another step and the house cracked sharply. I hopped backwards onto the safe side, the part of the house I had begun to think of as the rock. The lifted side now seemed winged, at one with the hawks that glide on invisible currents up on this windy hill.

It took me a while to give up the illusion of flight. But as the summer passed, the house rested well on its balancing beam and, as we dug and filled in the new foundation, I walked about upstairs, its airy underlayment all but forgotten.

In late August, a forecast for a hurricane hustled us to conclusion. The foundation had long since cured and new supports had been added. The beam could be removed now. Ethan returned with his excavator and his helper, Mel. The hurricane lurked to our south, a wobbling corkscrew on the weather map that gave our operation an additionally dramatic edge. An apprehensive audience of one, I took a seat in the field across the road. Ethan climbed up into his excavator. Mel was at ground level to guide the beam with his hands. With care and precision, they labored in the early evening light, the beam moving out from under the floorboards with the speed of the setting sun. At last, it swung free of my house, which now stood solid and proud on its new foundation.

Ethan cut the gas to the engine of his big machine and the air went silent. Ever the articulate woodsman, he turned toward me where I sat in the field and, with a grin, he raised his thumb into the fresh breeze.

ஃ *A Russian Year*

To do over this house, and do it the way I wanted to, it had to be done in stages, or I should say, has to be, as it won't be complete for many years to come. In this fashion, each segment becomes a whole and the process becomes a complete renewal.

In the ideal world, I would have lived elsewhere while this house was being pulled apart and put back together but that would have required more funds than I had. And so, in the late fall of my first year here, it did not seem quite so far-fetched to think that I could live in the back of the el while the work was being done. The el was built directly on the ground, back in the 1800s, and never could accommodate ductwork from the furnace, which was in the front part of the house. That there might be insulation was a fantasy. Electric heaters ran along the baseboards and there was a chimney.

I used the electric heat for a few weeks and then got my electric bill. In shock, I shut them down as well. I could tough it out. I'd lived through cold before. The woodstove would provide plenty of heat.

Cold, though, is like the pain of an excruciating injury or of childbirth. Once it's over, our memories can't seem to retain what it was like, how bad it really was.

A protective measure, no doubt, but I can't seem to shed the memory of how cold it was in this house that first winter. It was a gradual squeeze, a slowly closing vise. The autumn was not so bad, a kind of tease that lulled me into false confidence. Arising in the morning and quickly donning layers of ascendingly bulky woolens, I felt perhaps my worries had been almost silly. The fire in the woodstove was cheerful and a small fan moved heat to the next room. November was a cinch. December, not so bad. But the wood was getting low by then. I couldn't believe how fast I was pushing wood through that stove. On the coldest nights, the cold seemed to suck the warmth out of the stove. I felt I could sit on top of it and still not be warm. By January, I began using the hot water bottle in bed, as my aunt had suggested. That helped. In fact, the bed, with its flannel sheets and billowing down comforter, became a refuge of sorts. Add the hot water bottle at my feet and it was a place I never wanted to leave.

Sometime in late January, maybe early February, I began to feel as if nothing could warm me. Nothing. When the winds came up, which was frequently if not all the time, the curtains blew out as if from a summer's breeze through an open window. I spent as much time as I could in warm places like libraries and in the homes of friends. But worry about the possibility of freezing pipes kept me from staying away very long. I ate my dinners quickly (appreciating, for the first time, my grandmother's insistence on warming the plates) and then went to bed, the only place where I could truly feel warm. "How do you stay warm?" concerned friends would ask. "I go to bed," was my only answer.

One night, in utter desperation, I unearthed every spare throw rug from my storage boxes and, armed with a staple gun, I went about covering the rattly, single pane windows, in hopes of stopping the wind from coming in. I hung a heavy tapestry in the doorway that went from one room to the next. Thus covered, the darkness seemed complete. During the day, in the other part of the house, saws whirred and screw guns yelped. A whole new world was being created. New windows were shouldered into place. The light from the mountain streamed into the place that would someday be my home. Downstairs in my dungeon, I could hardly believe that I would ever live anywhere but there.

I remember feeling utterly pessimistic, hopelessly trapped, in spite of the very real and explicit evidence that my lot would change, and change soon. I found myself wondering how people who live desperate lives can ever muster the courage to free themselves. What extraordinary vision they must have to see themselves elsewhere, to *move* themselves elsewhere. How difficult is this thing called hope. I called it my year as a Russian peasant and, in spite of what they say about our inability to remember pain, I won't soon forget that cold.

ॐ *Night Sky*

T HE VIEW OF THE NIGHT SKY up here on the hill is so spectacular that two of my neighbors have taken note of it in naming their places. One is called Skyfield; the other Sky Hill. It took living here to understand the effect that a clear night sky can have.

An old friend, from a distant city, came to visit me soon after I moved here. He is a seer, a practicing reader of the stars, and he was anxious to see this wide view of the heavens that I had told him about. His visit fell on the night of the new moon, the darkest night of the month — the darkest night for us but the brightest night for the stars. When darkness had fallen completely, we walked out to the rise in the hill, the highest point here, and stood in the black stillness. As our eyes adjusted, we heard only the deafening quiet of the night, a quiet so complete, it seemed to reverberate around us. Overhead arched the great sparkling dome of the universe. Philip knew all the celestial configurations and with the patience of a professor, he pointed out each one. Even though I could not always follow the careful lines his finger drew, he slowly located each member of our night family. Orion. Perseus. Venus. After he had found all his old friends, we stood in silence for a long time, heads thrown back, oblivious to the cold. We had begun to travel into that timeless and mysterious place beyond our immediate world, that place that leaves us slightly in awe of our smallness.

My father, in his letters written home during World War II, used the night sky as a touchstone, the one thing he kept in common with the woman he hoped to marry. In the night sky my father found a place that banished climate and seasons, language and time zones, war and hate. Looking up from his tent pitched on a dark hill in North Africa, he watched the stars and the moon and then, the next morning, he wrote to my mother, half a world away, "I saw our moon last night and knew that you would soon see it too. I feel closer to you, for that moon."

The night sky, with all its sparkling constellations, is indeed the one unchanging aspect of our planet, the only physical terrain we share with other nations. I remember distinctly the first time I discovered the beauty of the night sky on this hill, the first time I realized why my neighbors had named their places with reverence to the sky. When I first moved here, there were a seemingly unending array of problems to be dealt with: broken pipes, a faltering foundation, insufficient heat, an overwhelming amount of debris from a devastating ice storm, a barn that had begun to collapse. The list was long and my resources were short. Each problem represented a puzzle and I lay awake, many nights, hoping for solutions that would not drive me into bankruptcy. One night these difficulties pressed in to an almost unbearable degree. It was a very dark night in January and I was very cold, staying deep under the covers. I turned this way and that but sleep would not come. At last, I got up and walked down the hall. One of the windows in the bathroom had a broken pane and I went over to it and with a towel, I tried to stem the flow of cold air. But my attention was instead drawn outside, way outside, up into the darkness where the stars virtually burned toward earth. The beauty was so startling, I remember saying, "Oh!", out loud, into the silence of that difficult night. The stars shimmered in their places, each one distinct, each one representing an eternity of its own. I knew at once why I was here.

Whether from a tent in Africa during a world war or from a cold farmhouse on a New Hampshire hill at the teetering end of the 20th century, we need these celestial guides to keep us from despair. The stars tell us other things, too, but maybe the most important thing that they tell us is how close we really are to each other.

✸ *My Winter Garden*

IN MID-WINTER, windows become of interest. Back in the 1970s, we were bombarded with frightening information such as the statement that 40% of a house's heat is lost through its single pane windows. And so we endeavored to change that and now most of us have windows that are double or triple glazed, windows thicker and more efficient than walls. This is an old house so, short of replacing all the windows, which would likely cost more than the house itself, storm windows were added, the newer version with screens that slide down in the summer and extra windows that slide into place in winter. These do the job, though they are not as sleek as new double-glazed windows. I am snug behind them in the winter and I don't need extra sweaters anymore when I sit near a window. So, they are efficient and I am warmer and my heating bills are lower. But there is one thing that I miss, with these window walls: ice flowers.

Back before the windows were changed, incredible works of art grew on the inside of my windows, especially at night, when the temperature dropped below zero. I could watch the pattern grow, tiny needles of ice making their way across the glass, like brushstrokes creating an incredible silver canvas of cold.

On warm days, the ice would melt and water would bead up on the pane. But at night, the painting would return with the cold, and we would read the patterns like clouds, seeing feathers and ferns, lace and doilies, palm fronds, star bursts and pinwheels, birds in flight. Through this windowpane fantasy, ice and cold became a master of creativity.

I discovered that if I scratched a message onto the glass with the slightest of razor blades, the hoary words would appear overnight. Or if I washed the windows with a certain stroke, the next night's pattern would follow that stroke. I used to look forward to the coldest nights because I knew that in the morning, when the sun came up and shone through the bedroom window, there would be a brand new design. It somehow made the cold more bearable. I would lie there, still snug in bed, and watch the light of the sun bring the night's frost painting alive. I thought of this window as my winter garden, where blooms came faster and more dramatically than any flower ever could.

Years ago, in Vermont, there was a man who was fascinated by snowflakes, fascinated enough to try to preserve them. William Alwyn Bentley would walk out into a fresh snowstorm in a heavy coat and stand with his arms outstretched, catching the snowflakes on a board covered with black cloth. Using his carefully constructed, blanketed camera rig, he'd photograph the flakes. A frail little man with a bristlebrush mustache who did his work in his farmyard and in his cold shed and inside his farmhouse, he became known as "Snowflake Bentley" and, on par with some of the most notable scientists, he changed forever the way we think about snow and about cold. Bentley photographed not just snowflakes, but anything cold: frost, hail, rime, sleet, and dew. He also photographed frost patterns on windowpanes. With no scientific training whatsoever, he carried this hobby on for over forty years and when he died in 1931, he left behind him more than 5,000 photographs of snowflakes. It is because of his work that we now maintain, with some certainty, that no two snowflakes are alike. Scientists used these photographs to further their knowledge of snow and cold. Lace makers used these photographs to create new designs for tablecloths and window curtains. Tiffany's used these photographs to create designs for gold pendants and brooches. I use these photographs to remember the gift of our window-born frost gardens and a time when we could wake up in the morning and see the beauty of the cold from beneath our blankets, before we had to emerge into it.

✣ *Gideon's Labors*

WITH THIS FARM came four hay fields, each separated by a row of trees and hedge. The fields are small, four or five acres each, but the hay that grows on them is good, or so I have been told. Soon after I took possession of the farm, the need to find someone to hay my fields rose to the top of my "to do" list.

Open fields are uncommon here, as forests rule, so I thought that finding someone to cut this hay would be easy. But the number of open fields seemed to be in an opposing ratio with the number of farmers, now far fewer than the fields.

One phone call led to another. Finally, I called a man who lives more than twenty miles from here. His name was Gideon, a farmer with a day job. He was doing whatever he could to keep his herd, which his wife tended while he was at work. In spite of the distance and his difficult schedule, when I asked him if he'd like the hay here, he said, "Yes, I'd like that."

So when the hay was tall, Gideon came one evening with his blue Ford tractor and the cutter on a trailer. In the west field, he unloaded and began to couple the two together. The

machinery was old. He was still dressed in street shoes, pre-
sumably having come from his job. I watched from the window as he hoisted himself up into the tractor seat, started the
throaty old engine, and began to cut the first big loop. He got
halfway around the edge of the field when I heard the tractor
engine die. By this time, the sun was setting. Gideon left then,
the tractor and cutter still in its tracks, a single swath cut in
the high grass which rose like a fence between my house and
my neighbor's.

The next day it rained. In the evening, Gideon returned
with a friend. They wore black rain slickers and boots and by
the light of Gideon's truck headlights, they worked on the cutter, which apparently needed a bearing. It was dark and the rain
was coming down at an angle when he came to the back door
to tell me this news. He said he'd be back.

There is a rhythm to haying that I have always loved. The
grass grows tall. When the moment is right, the farmer comes
to hay and when he leaves, the load of bales high on his wagon,
the field is like a swept house. I always feel a tremendous sense
of relief when the haying is done. My experience with Gideon
was less satisfying. There was a long period of time when the
tractor sat in the field and I began to despair that the field
would be left half cut through the winter.

Eventually Gideon returned. The bearing was installed
and he continued with the task. But there were other problems.
Bad weather and more engine troubles but, perhaps more than
anything, what Gideon did not have was time. In haying, tim-
ing is everything, my husband used to say, and Gideon's time

was clearly not his own. He could barely get here before the sun set or the clouds released their rain.

One evening, he came for the last of the hay, which sat in bales in the field. The sky was threatening and I went out and asked if he wanted me to help throw bales onto his truck, to beat the rain. But Gideon just waved back and said, "No, thanks, we're all set."

How he did it, I don't know, but he got the last of the bales up onto the truck. With a toot of his horn, he was gone. Some while later, the rain began to fall, gently. The fields were smooth and open, a clean sweep. For the first time since late June, I could see my neighbor's house. I was grateful to Gideon for his labors and I felt relieved, that these fields had survived another year in the absence of farmers.

ॐ *Baked Earth*

THE VILLAGE HERE is all bricks. The old woolen mill is made of bricks, the picking and sorting house is made of bricks, the church is made of bricks, the store is made of bricks, the boarding house is made of bricks. It's a brick mill village and until I moved up here to the farm, I never stopped to think about where all the bricks came from.

The fields on this farm are wide and open and crested like upturned shallow bowls. The sun bakes here all day long. Hay grows agreeably in the fields and once, I am told, corn grew just as well, as did flax and even soybeans. One section, though, is steep and broken by outcrops of rock. On a walk through these fields, Chick Colony, whose family ran the mills in the 19th and 20th centuries, and who himself now runs a business in town selling looms and weaving supplies, pointed to a pile of rubble and said, "That's where the old brick mill was."

It was like an essential truth had been demonstrated to me. *Of course!* The bricks had to come from *somewhere!* And the somewhere was *here*, on this hill above town, an easy downhill slide for the wagons that carted the bricks into town. Almost at once, I could imagine that early industry, the bricks, that by logic, had to have come before the mills. I could imagine the smoke coming up out of the big kilns and, visible along the brow of the hill, stacks of bricks ready to build an industry apart from their own.

Another reason why the bricks and the mill on the hill made sense was what I would discover as I began to garden up here: the soil. It's the densest clay I have ever worked. Thick and heavy as cream cheese, the soil does not break or crumble in my hands or even to the work of my fork. For this earth to yield, it virtually has to be cut. To make anything grow in my fledgling garden, early efforts included mixing lots of peat moss and compost. I began to feel I was fighting a riptide. I started thinking about the bricks, wondering why they had stopped making them here. Maybe once the town was built, there wasn't much further need for bricks. Still, it seemed like a resource lying fallow. I thought further of the friends I have nearby who work in clay, and wondered if the soil could be useful to them. But when I asked, they told me that this raw earth was not refined enough. Screened and sealed, their clay comes to them in plastic bags, imported from exotic places.

But bricks are not celadon bowls. Bricks can be made right out of the earth. I have seen the way they make old bricks, cutting the clay into the standard shape and firing trays of these soft forms into the hard shapes we know as bricks. During that red-hot process, they turn the wonderful colors that we think of as "brick red." All bricks are is baked earth.

One of the first things I did here was to have the old chimney taken down. It could no longer be used safely and I had plans for a different chimney. And so one day a crew of strapping young men came and, using sledgehammers, they whacked away at the big stout stack that leaned against the west side of the house. They heaved the old bricks into their truck as they worked and when they were done, they started to drive away with the big load. "No! Wait!" I cried, running after them. I asked them to dump the load out behind the barn, which they did. And for the next several weeks, I began each day by going out behind the barn and sorting through that big pile, tossing the broken ones aside but, when I came to a brick that was good and whole, I'd chip off any mortar and stack it neatly with the others I'd salvaged.

I now have a decent pile of bricks, a checkerboard of colors that range from a soft pink to a deep burnt red, waiting to find a project. They're old, some of them as old as this farm, and they are of this earth.

❧ The Old Apple Tree

THE APPLE TREE THAT STANDS on the far side of the driveway has been here for probably 150 years or more. With apple trees, it's hard to tell how old they are as they don't so much grow tall as they absorb age into their joints, which swell and twist. In the case of this tree, the joints tell me that it has lived through much, that it has blossomed and given fruit and then turned to winter's stone, over and over, through many chapters of our history. Surely, for instance, this tree bore fruit through the Civil War.

Not long ago, I met an old man at a wedding. He inquired where I lived and I told him I had bought Mary's farm up on top of Beech Hill. His rheumy eyes grew animated with recognition, oh, yes, he said, he had spent many a summer day on that farm. He especially remembered the lightning in this high place. "Does the telephone still jump off the wall in a lightning storm?" he asked. I told him I'd never seen that happen, but, I added, perhaps that is because there is no longer a phone on the wall, only a cordless that I carry from room to room. "Well," he went on, still clearly in the grip of these summer memories, "I can remember one storm, oh, it was a doozy. The cow was standing under the apple tree and a bolt came down and struck her. Dead as a mackerel!"

That cow may have been dead as a mackerel but the tree survived. The tree survived until ten days after I bought the farm. Ice, the silent killer, hung itself so heavily on its branches that it split this fabulous ancient tree into three pieces, one collapsing on the roof of the tractor barn, another onto the little greenhouse and across the driveway. When the ice melted, the tree was splayed across the landscape as if it had simply given up and opened itself up to the sky.

One sucker remained. By the standard of that particular tree, the sucker was a very slender trunk. But, by the standards of the average tree, it was a hefty contender on the property. I hired Dan Washburn, a ringer for Paul Bunyan if I ever saw one, to clean up the remains of the tree. I asked him what the chances were for the lone sucker to survive and he stood and surveyed the wreck for a long moment before he answered, "Not so good. But maybe if you prop it up, it might do better." He cut a good strong limb from the wreckage, with a short crotch at the top, and he wedged it under the leaning survivor.

I was anxious for some part of that tree to survive. The hints of history were nice but the apples' legend was even stronger. Many neighbors had told me that the fruits of that tree were extraordinary, worth the price of the farm, one of them told me, only slightly in jest. Other unsolicited testimonies included one from the man who painted my kitchen. He told me, somewhat sheepishly, that he had been working next door a few years ago and at lunch he had walked down to Mary's and stolen an apple from her tree. These were not perfect, produce aisle apples, but rather distinguished by worm holes and offset cores. "I've never, ever had a better apple," he said.

If it was ever known what kind of apples this tree gave, that fact has been lost to its long history.

In the spring after the ice storm, I watched that tree anxiously. The greening came late but nonetheless, it came. The leaves were sparse, though, and there were no blossoms. Through the summer, it was anyone's guess whether the tree would revive or succumb. Spotted leaves and no fruit were the only reports I could give. The sturdy crutch my tree man had stuck under its lean had nearly taken root in the ground.

A year of seasons passed. I can never quite tell when a tree is going to blossom; the flowers always take me by surprise. And so it was with this new tree that had sprung like a flag from ruins of the old. This, after all, was the tree that survived when the cow succumbed. One May morning, I looked out and the propped-up sucker was snow white with blossoms. In the fall, I tasted the apples for the first time. If these were the apples that went to war in the pocket of a young soldier, it was a war well fought. And well won.

✣ The Scent of Summer

WHEN I WAS GROWING UP, my mother had a clothesline a good distance from the house, beside a grove of trees. This was a matter of modesty as both my father and my mother seemed to agree that the business of hanging out one's laundry exposed private items which one would just as soon not have the neighbors view. And so they positioned the clothesline discreetly.

When my mother's front-loading Westinghouse finished its cycle, she and I would walk down to the clothesline together, carrying the clothes basket between us, and hang the clean laundry out in the sun. My father had built the frame from cedar posts and pine boards and strung several lengths of clothesline between. My mother instructed as I pinned the clothes to the white roping: hang the bluejeans from their cuffs (after giving them a good shake to snap out any wrinkles) and pull the pockets inside out so they will dry too; hang the shirts from their collars; socks should be hung from the toe end. I recall feeling connected to each piece of clothing, whether it was mine or someone else's in the family, as I hung it in the hot sun. It took both of us to hang the sheets, extending them tightly. And while we worked, my mother and I often talked in ways we did not at other times. When everything was hung with its best advantage toward the sun, we would leave, the laundry swaying gently in the summer air. At the end of the day, we would return to the dry and fragrant clothing, as good as any ripe harvest.

There was a special scent that came out of those clothes, especially the sheets. "Smells of the sun," my mother would say. I wondered how anything as invisible and intangible as sunlight could have an odor. Nothing else I could ever think of smelled like the sun. But I loved getting into bed at night with those clean sheets, and the scent of summer.

At that time in the 1950s and 1960s, everyone had a clothesline and when we were out in the car, we enjoyed pointing out particularly colorful or interesting displays. To us, clotheslines offered clues to the mystery of each house we passed. One old lady lived alone and her bloomers often puffed out in the breeze in a sad, solitary sort of way. I had never seen her but I had those bloomers to start my story about who she was and what her life was all about. Some women seemed to take pride in the way their clothes were arranged on the line, almost as if the clothing sent signals that spoke of order and thought. Especially admirable were the ones who hung the clothes in categories and ascending sizes, with the children's socks gradually expanding to the adult sizes and the underwear as well. This always amused my mother, who felt that there were limits to how much time she would spend on such a task. And yet we enjoyed the precise, almost militaristic displays. Most of all, we enjoyed the colors, a palette like no other.

My mother, bless her soul, never owned a clothes dryer in her long life. It was not an economic decision, particularly — though she did enjoy saving money — but the whole idea of clothes dryers seemed to puzzle her. She knew, for instance, that many articles of clothing came out of the dryer damaged or reduced in size. While she pondered all this, the clothesline gradually became extinct. In fact, there are ordinances in more and more places that outlaw clotheslines as being unsightly. Perhaps. But what about all those insights into our neighbors' lives and habits?

I, in my modern life, have taken clothes dryers for granted. They are handy and convenient. But I've always maintained a clothesline, and use it when the weather is right. When I moved here to Mary's farm, I noticed that the clothesline was in a place that was not, in fact, particularly sunny. But, like my mother's, it was hidden. I canvassed the property for a sunnier location. There was really only one place: beside the horse barn, in full view of the road. On good days, I carry the clothes basket out to the line and pin my laundry into the sun. By afternoon it is dry and scented with summer's warmth. I sometimes think I see cars slow as they pass the house, checking out the clothes and seeing what they might have to say about me.

❧ *Weather or Not*

NEW ENGLAND IS NOT KNOWN for its hurricanes. We had our 1938 whopper, which had been predicted as nothing more than "strong winds." Bricks, firewood, even apples from the ripening trees became bullets, puncturing walls, felling cattle. After the storm had passed, farmers 100 miles inland told of saltwater streaks on their windows. Nearly 700 people were killed by this unforecast nightmare. Three hundred million trees were lost or damaged, giving rise to the term "hurricane lumber."

With each hurricane season that comes, there lurks the possibility of a rerun. The weather channels track them, the Glorias and the Bobs, as if they were the criminally insane, escaped from their hold. On the nightly news, forecasters pinpoint the storm, days, sometimes weeks away, give it a name, and mark its progress. Like an unfolding drama, we watch the great wheel of catastrophe that rolls up out of Africa, careens through the Caribbean, and wobbles onward up the east coast. With the camera's eye, the TV tells the story, so far. In the tropics, roofs lie scattered. Palm trees bend and touch the ground. Waves crash through picture windows. But Septembers come and go and the storms blow away or change course before they reach us here in southwestern New Hampshire.

Last year, though, they felt sure we were in for it. It was early September, a beautiful mild time here. We had not yet had a frost. The air was close. Sitting outside in the evening still seemed like the best idea we could think of. It seemed much too early to carry in the lawn furniture and evacuate the porch. But Floyd, an enormous coil of thick clouds with a hole in the center, was on every channel we can get. "This is a huge storm," the forecasters admonished. And the map showed its fury could reach from Maryland to Maine.

Inside, I flicked on the evening news. Aerial photos showed a traffic jam leaving the coast of North Carolina like a line into infinity. Heavy surf crashed through the living rooms of oceanside cottages.

In my TV-charged imagination, I pictured uprooted trees and felled power lines; my innocent lawn furniture became lethal weapons. And so in came the chairs. And the tables and the birdhouses and feeders. Even the wind chimes, which are made of clay and have the contemplative sound of Buddhist bells, were taken in. Like a bankrupt cafe, our summery outdoor living space went dead. I walked around the house and barn one last time and on the final circuit, hefted the birdbath and set it in a horse stall in the barn and latched the doors.

That night, it rained. There was a bit of wind. And, in the morning, the sun lit up the garden. Could that have been it? On the television, the big wooly wheel of Floyd was turning toward the Maritimes. That evening, listening to the radio, I heard a man who had evacuated from Florida say he would never, never leave again, no matter if he had to be arrested. His home in Florida was completely untouched by Floyd, which collided with the coast of North Carolina and then veered out to sea. The people who suffered most were the inland farmers of North Carolina who were completely unprepared for the flooding that followed the storm. It rained for days and their houses filled like empty buckets. In spite of the days and days of watchful advisement, no one warned this would happen.

Do we really know how to do anything but photograph the weather? In the clear, post-Floyd morning air, I set the chairs outside again and hung the feeders and the wind chimes. There would be another month of summer, surely. I carried dinner outside on trays and we ate into the warm darkness, to the sound of the crickets. I felt a sense of relief mixed with sadness for those who had been so devastated by the unpredicted floods. A week or so later, I woke in the night to the howl of high winds. Rain rushed against the windows with hurricane force. The house timbers creaked and wind chimes rang wild. In the morning, the lawn chairs were scattered in the field, as if from a night of reckless partying. My wind chimes lay in pieces on the ground. The forecast had been for rain, some wind.

Dial 911

A FEW YEARS AGO, the decree came down that we should be able to dial 911 in New Hampshire. We have never had 911 but instead we dialed an entire seven digit number which connected to a switchboard in Keene, the biggest town around. The fellows there would signal our local fire department or police, which, in the case of Mike, our one and only man in blue, sometimes required that his wife fetch him off his tractor or out of the hay barn. This worked fairly well. In a town with a head count of a thousand, we don't have daily or even weekly emergencies. The police report for our annual meeting runs one page, as does the report from the fire chief.

So when the word filtered around that they were going to change some of the road names so that 911 could find us, some of us were mystified. We all seemed to be able to find our way well enough and certainly our police and fire departments know where most of us are. Their explanation was that some of the roads around here have names that resemble other names. Old Harrisville Road is sometimes confused with New

Harrisville Road. And, since there are several roads that lead to the next town of Hancock, there are therefore several Hancock Roads.

Pretty soon, I received in the mail a letter informing me of my new address. Instead of Old Harrisville Road, my address was now 33 Mason Road. They chose the name of Mason because it was Benjamin Mason who built this house in 1762. I have not yet figured out how they decided I would be number 33. I'm one of only two houses on the one mile length of what is now Mason Road.

I was also asked to nail large numbers onto the front of my house. It felt odd when I did so, since there is not another house in sight.

Soon after that, UPS and FedEx started calling to say that they had attempted to deliver a package but could not find 33 Mason Road. So I would tell them it's really Old Harrisville Road and that seemed to clear things up. Until their next attempt at delivery. It wasn't just me, I discovered. When I'd be out for walks, delivery vans and repair trucks would slow to a stop beside me and the puzzled drivers, map in hand, would ask me where this road was or that road, all of them new to the system. I began to feel a sense of alarm. Apparently the new names were not on the old maps.

Recently my phone went out in a storm. I reported it and was told it would be repaired by 8 that evening. But 8 came and went and my phone was still dead. I went to a friend's house to call again. After being put on hold for an extended length of time, the lady from the phone company came back on the line, sounding somewhat chagrined. "I know this sounds weird," she said. "But the reason we couldn't fix your phone is that we couldn't find you."

When the phone company cannot find me, I am worried. I've not yet had an occasion to dial 911 and hope I don't have to. To me, it seems almost absurd to think simply dialing three digits on a telephone can be more efficient than our old system, even if it meant getting Mike off his tractor. I'm still not convinced that it can.

✣ *The Purple Line*

I F Y O U C O U L D L O O K O U T my front window, you
would see a broad, humped hay field. Beyond it is a
stretch of forest, mostly tall oak trees and some pine. And then
rising above both is the mountain, Mount Monadnock, a long
stretch of rock much wider than it is high, its rocky peak
exposed like the blade of an old knife.

If things had gone as planned, what you would see out
this window would be a highway, at least two lanes, perhaps
four, and what you would hear would not be the silence but
the steady whine of cars and trucks passing at a high rate of
speed. The proposal came almost thirty years ago. I did not
know Mary then — I did not even live in this town — but I
know that she fought very hard to keep her fields from becoming pavement. At that time, her farm was growing hay and
some corn. Once I arrived here in town, some ten years after
that first proposal, I remember the meetings and the climate
of fear that prevailed all through this town. Bumper stickers
proclaimed "NO EAST-WEST HIGHWAY" and talk of the
road was never far from anyone's tongue.

In the newspaper and elsewhere, the state published a map, with lines proposing various ways that the highway could get around the mountain — one of the big obstacles to a speedy passage from one side of the state to the other. On that map, an ominous purple line ran smack through Mary's farm. And, though there were several alternate bypasses proposed, that particular route was the one state officials thought would work best. A book could be written about this more-than-twenty-year battle to keep the road from coming through.

Oddly, what the highway proposal produced in this town was history, or a study of it. I'm sure we would have found our way to our history eventually but the highway mandate pushed us along. As it turned out, the town, with its unspoiled brick mill buildings ringed by lakes, had enough history to fill books. And Mary's farm, they were pretty sure, was the most historically significant farm in the district, and likely the oldest. Dating from 1762, the farm was here long before the town. Working with what documents they had and with the memories of the elders of the town, they discovered that the farm had been producing hay and corn and timber since before the Revolution. In a sense, the farm and the Mason family who lived here helped support the developing town, which was incorporated in 1870, more than a century after this house was built. As the mills sprang up in the village, this farm first produced bricks with which to build the buildings, then wool to sell to the blanket mills. The farm raised beef to feed the mill workers, who lived in boarding houses beside the mill. In the little barn, around which Mary planted a great variety of lilacs, there was a shop where leather shoes were made.

The house, from which I write this, was moved to this location from the top of the hill and eventually a variety of outbuildings — including a laundry and an outhouse — were linked out to the big barn. These connecting outbuildings were taken down in the 1940s but for the purposes of the historical study, a drawing was made of what the original house looked like. (More than anything, it must have looked like a long train, chugging toward the mountain.) The information about Mary's farm was just one small part of a big packet that was put together and sent to the powers that be in Washington D.C., in hopes of placing us on the National Register of Historic Places.

It was not just history, of course, that kept the road from coming through. There was also this rugged climate that gives us ice when our neighbors just a mile down the road have rain, the climate that gives us gale-force winds when our friends in the village only feel a stiff breeze. We can always be grateful to those who came before us for their efforts, which, often enough, we can see. But in this case the desired result was nothing. What is most striking to me today is that when I look out at those green fields and tell visitors that at one time, this was all but certainly to be a major highway, they are amazed. And they would never know this if someone did not tell them. Sometimes the most interesting parts of our history are what did not happen.

ॐ *The First Wolf*

AROUND HERE, THE STORY of the wolves is pretty well known. This house was built just after the French and Indian wars. Peace had finally come and folks felt safe to begin to settle the land that had so recently been a war zone. We all face the mountain, a great long wedge that both divides and bonds together all the towns that revolve around it. Even as these early men and women built their barns, sheep and calves were regularly lost to wolves that lived on the mountain. This loss must have been no small matter to those who kept these farms. Living here, with all the conveniences available to me, I often think of those who came before me and the challenges they faced through the short summers and the very long winters.

Bounties were offered on wolf scalps, and I know from reading historical records that the man who built this house was among those who brought wolf scalps to the state for pay — eight dollars for an old wolf and five for a young one. The wolves, they knew, lived in the thick forest near the top of the mountain.

Sometime around 1800, the mountain caught on fire, though it is uncertain whether it started spontaneously or whether it was set, perhaps by an angry farmer. In any case, the mountain burned for three weeks. One farmer said that the fire was so bright that, at night, he could read his newspaper by its light.

When the smoke cleared, the mountain had a new face: sheer rock at the top. Described as "nearly volcanic," the fire scorched the earth and left the rock itself molten in places. The trees which had forested the top fell into a great pile, creating the perfect haven for wolves and their cubs. For the next twenty years, the wolf population increased alongside the farmers' anguish. In 1820, the farmers deliberately kindled another fire, burning the wolves' dens inside this great stack of dead wood. Again, the conflagration extended several miles across the mountain's flanks, pumping smoke and flame. A heavy rain extinguished the blaze and when the embers died, it was evident that the wolves were gone.

Except for one. Known as the Lone Wolf or the Last Wolf, he was hunted ferociously and the bounty was increased to $20, a huge sum in those days. At last, farmers from all over banded together into a human chain, cornering the wolf in a small field. It is recorded that they fired fifty shots but the wily creature escaped to another meadow where a young man named Nathaniel Stanley felled him. The crowd brought the carcass into the common, amid the cheers of local people. No wolf has been seen here since.

We don't think much about wolves anymore. There is even talk of bringing them back, purposefully re-introducing them. Not that many years ago, someone reported seeing a coyote near the mountain. I recall that the sighting was dismissed, since, it was said, there are no coyotes here. Now, there are so many coyotes living on or near the mountain, they provide a kind of operatic background music as I go about my work. My ear is tuned to their cry, as a city dweller's might be to police sirens — the two sounds are remarkably similar.

Last summer, on my way up the steep hill that leads to this farm, a large animal crossed my path. I see coyotes probably more often than I see deer. This was not a coyote. It was bigger, with a lush gray coat. Its eyes were hauntingly light, like dimes. It struck me: could that have been a wolf? It vanished before I could really fasten my eyes on it and be sure. I called the game warden and questioned him. No, he said, they shot the last wolf almost 200 years ago. There are no wolves here.

Maybe, then, what I saw was not the last wolf, but the first.

৵ *Silent Storms* ·

THE FIRST TIME I EVER SAW the Northern Lights it was a very cold night in January. At that time in our youthful lives, my husband and I felt exhilarated by nights when the temperature fell below zero. It felt like a great challenge set before us. Often, we bundled in down coats and heavy boots and went for walks late on these cold nights. There was a stillness that settled with the cold and the snow under our boots squeaked loudly as we walked along the silent road. Once, on such a walk, well past midnight, we looked up into the north sky and were startled to see sheets of green, wavering like flags. We were stunned and grateful we had each other to know we were not seeing things. It was only later that we realized what we had seen that night were the Northern Lights. I thought these phenomena were only visible in Alaska and the northern parts of Canada. But apparently not. Twenty-five years went by before I saw them again.

This time it was at the end of October of last year. I was driving home from a late night of teaching in Boston. As I drove, I saw in the distance what I thought were searchlights sweeping the sky. I thought perhaps it was a car dealer in Fitchburg trying to attract attention to a special sale, though it seemed kind of late for that. The lights were white and they appeared to sweep the sky, back and forth. But after I passed through Fitchburg, the lights were still strong in the sky. It wasn't until I crossed the border into New Hampshire that I realized I was seeing the *aurora borealis*. By the time I arrived home, where the night sky is black and unhampered by light pollution, the white lights had turned a soft pink.

The next day the newspaper reported a large solar storm had erupted on the sun and sent clouds of dust hurtling toward earth. These light shows had been seen all over the world, even as far south as Georgia. The report said that the storms would continue for several days. I was not teaching the next night so I planned to get up in the middle of the night to look for the lights. But the next evening, just after the sun set, I happened to step out into my driveway. It was sweater weather, but not very cold out yet. I looked to the west and saw waves of green and pink moving in the sky, like curtains puffed out by a summer breeze. I stood transfixed beneath this canopy of color. At the edge, great pillars of white light swayed back and forth in ecstatic motion. My dog, looking up, barked at what she had never seen before. Everything I thought I knew about the Northern Lights — that they appear only in the north sky, that they come on nights of extreme cold, that they happen only in the middle of the night — was proving false. I went inside to get my camera but by the time I got back, the show was over and darkness had settled back over the hill. Two

nights later, the lights returned, another majestic display fol-
lowing an early November sunset.

The Northern Lights are the result of huge storms on the
surface of the sun, explosions of a magnitude we cannot even
begin to comprehend. In the past, satellites have been damaged
by these eruptions and radio communications have been sev-
ered. The storms produce a speed and energy of highly violent
proportions. And yet, we will sleep through these catastrophic
intergalactic events if we aren't vigilant or lucky. To us, the
aurora borealis are silent, mystical pageants of great beauty and
peace. Standing there, under that unearthly illumination, I
could think of nothing but good, a reminder of the existence
of mystery and the inherent benevolence of the night sky.

ॐ The Philosophy of Drift

THERE'S A SAYING UP HERE in New England: if you don't like the weather, wait a minute and it will change. Usually, that's about right. But, a couple of winters ago, there was just one relentless ongoing aspect to our weather: snow. At its peak, the snow reached the second story windows here and the drifts were so high that one rose up outside my bedroom window like a tidal wave, complete with a curl at the top. As that particular storm began to wane, I walked into the room, saw the big wave coming at me from outside my window and almost died of heart failure.

Most of our winter storms are northeasters, which last two or three days. My house, perched as it is atop a high hill, became like a ship at sea in a furious storm. For days, it seemed, the dim light outside revealed only horizontal snow racing past the windows. The deafening sound of the wind — a cacophony of screaming, howling, whistling — kept me awake more than one night. During one storm, I watched in alarm as snow piled against the window pane like water rising. Daylight did not come through that window again for weeks.

Throughout it all, I sat here like a shipwrecked sailor, rationing supplies, keeping the bathtub filled with water and pushing wood through the woodstoves like food to hungry dogs. In the last, most astonishing storm, the man who plows my driveway had to give up after his plow broke — for the third time. When he called to tell me, I thought for a minute that I heard him weeping on the other end of the line. It didn't matter anyway, the snow from that storm was so deep and so dense, I had to hire a bucket loader to liberate me.

By March, there was great concern for roofs as the weight of the snow increased with each storm. I worried about my barn, an uncertain structure, which at this point in its ancient life is held together with a chain and a come-along. Roofs around the region were collapsing one after the other. Like some weird, snow-bidden choreography, several buildings in different towns went down all virtually at once. The fury of the storms on my hill apparently saved me. After each storm passed, I went out to survey my roofs and found not a flake of snow on any of them. The ferocious wind had a hidden kindness, carrying the great weight elsewhere.

At a certain point during the winter, the philosophy of drift became a topic of interest. Was that *real* snow that filled my windows and covered my doorways or had it simply drifted there? One of the local newspapers took the issue to task. They sent a reporter out to take random measurements of the snow and discovered that — *aha!* —instead of the four and five and six feet people were claiming, there was really only eighteen inches on the ground, eighteen inches of *actual* snow, snow that had not drifted or been pushed by a plow.

As I sat there in my snow-sealed room, I took the issue seriously. Was all this snow that surrounded me simply an illusion? Were the great piles that had buried all but my roofs a trick of wind and location? Did it matter? Like the legendary tree that falls in the woods — if we were not there to hear it fall, did it actually fall? — my snow was there whether it drifted there or not and the idea that there *really* was only eighteen inches on the ground amused me not even a little bit. That meant that the drift curling ominously outside my bedroom window was simply an exaggeration, moved there by a great wind. But — of course! And what of the snow that was not on my roofs but that had settled instead on the sagging roofs of the buildings that went down? If this was not real, I did not, at that point, really know what was.

ॐ *Under Cover*

ONE THING I NEVER HAD before moving here to Mary's farm was a garage. Growing up as I did in New Jersey, it seemed that every house had a garage, a thing taken for granted, just as every house had bedrooms and bathrooms. But the old farmhouses in New England did not incorporate housing for the car and such has been the case with every house I have lived in here. I became completely accustomed to having the car sit in the driveway. As a result, weather was always a factor. If I came home with a back seat full of groceries, they had to be carried in through whatever rain, snow, lightning, or high winds were happening at the time. Even apart from carrying anything indoors, if I came home in a storm, I had to make my way through it to get to the back door. Similarly, I had to shovel my way through snowdrifts or inch across sheets of ice to get to the car. And snow always needed to be cleaned off the car and ice needed to be chipped from the windshield before I could go anywhere. In summer, the car baked in the sun. And, because a huge pine tree loomed above the driveway, dots of sap became part of the car's patina.

In all that had to be considered and dealt with when I bought Mary's farm, I hardly noticed the garage, which was once the pig shed. Many years ago, the house, which is about 300 yards distant from the barn, was completely attached to the barn through a long series of sheds that ran between the house and the barn like a long train, with the house as engine and the barn as caboose. I suppose the theory was similar to what motivated architects to attach the modern garage to the modern house. The farmer did not want to have to go outside into the grips of a snowstorm or a driving rainstorm in order to feed his animals. But the sheds were rarely built with any real conviction and often the tie between house and barn became a sagging hammock that eventually gave way to the elements. The rest of the outbuildings that led to the barn here went that way but the one closest to the kitchen was salvaged and revamped for use as a two-car garage. I use this now for my one car, my tractor, my wood supply and various and sundry items such as the battery charger, the garden tools, the saw I use to cut up kindling, and the Shaker woodstove that hasn't yet found a home inside the house.

In summer, a family of barn swallows nests in the rafters. I have to remember to leave the garage door open at all times so the mother has access to her babies. In fact, since the nests are directly above my windshield, which results in something of a mess, I tend not to use the garage at that time of year. It's in the winter that the garage becomes almost sacred to me. Several winters ago, when the snows were up to the second story windows, I went out to open the garage door, an effort that required the strength of Hercules. When the door finally rose, I was faced with a wall of snow that went up to my nose.

That's the kind of experience that leaves me wondering how I ever managed without a garage, a vital place wherein baby birds are born, cars are coddled, tractors are welcomed out of the weather, cordwood is left to dry, and windshields need never be scraped (except at swallow time). I know there are more luxurious garages, with automatic door openers, sheetrock walls, and even heat. But I'm happy for the shelter of this old pig shed, very happy indeed.

❧ *Another Year of Mercy*

I'VE BEEN TOLD THAT the barn behind the house here is older than the house, which dates to 1762. Usually a family builds the house before the barn, though I suppose there are always exceptions and no one was recording what the Masons did when they came here from Massachusetts in the lull between the French and Indian War and the American Revolution. Whatever happened with the house, I know for sure that the barn is older than this nation.

The building is tall, 30 × 45, and built on the ground. Inside, the timbers that support the structure are blonde, wide at the top and tapered toward the bottom: gunstock posts made of oak. The tenons that connect the posts and the beams are big as corncobs and they too are still light-colored, as if they were hammered in there yesterday.

Stepping into this barn is like stepping into an American history book. In there, I cannot help but think of the men who carved these posts out of trees, which grew, undoubtedly, very near to where the barn now sits. On the ground floor, there are two big windowless box stalls on one side and three smaller ones on the other. Each of these smaller stalls has a window looking east. In the center is a wide aisle that runs the length of the building — at each end are doorways broad enough to drive a wagon through, which I'm sure was what happened most every day, the horses harnessed and hitched in the shelter of the barn and then driven out into the field, where hay or corn was picked up and brought back in through the other side. In this barn, roosters strutted, hens pecked, horses snuffled, cows were milked, and hay was thrown aloft. Generations of farmers stamped snow off their boots or wiped sweat from their brows, entering the building where their business took place, every day of the year.

It's quiet now. Leaning as it does to the north and east, the barn has taken on a poetic profile, the sort that photographers and painters love to capture. Inside, the stalls harbor many things. One stall is piled with a collection of shutters and windows, likely saved from the last renovation, which I believe took place in the 1950s. Another has boxes of saved magazines, all of them swollen and yellowed with years of sun and moisture, and yet another has a hodgepodge of old wooden kitchen chairs and an enamel kitchen stove, missing the lids.

Since I bought Mary's farm, I've managed well with the house, some months counting out my last nickels in order to get done what needs to be done. But the barn has suffered and I've only been able to take two swipes at saving it, more triage than repair: when the wide expanse of the back door frame began to sag, a metal bar was hastily wedged into place. And in the corner afflicted with dry rot, we cinched the buckled post back into place using a chain and a come-along, which remain tight. These measures may buy time until I can afford more.

Winters are what bring these structures down. The winds and the heavy snows combine to defeat their heritage. Throughout each winter, I look out my window to the barn and say silent prayers. In April, I watch the snow retreat and whisper thanks for another year of mercy.

Because of what the barn has to say, I want it to live another century. I dream of sheep in the stalls, the fragrance of lanolin and hay and manure scenting the aisle, and red-backed chickens in the coop, muttering and squawking and flapping when I walk in with the grain.

ॐ *Still Standing*

WHENEVER I LOOK at the old maps for these backwoods areas, I am drawn to the tiny black squares that mark where houses once were or still are. Usually, even if the house is gone, the cellar holes are still there and these have often provided intrigue for me and a friend looking for old glass or antique implements, treasures to take home, and also small clues to the life that once moved inside the vanished structure.

A rusted piece of an old iron stove leans against my stone wall. I found that in a cellar hole in the middle of the woods, where it was hard to imagine a house had ever been. Where was the road? No answers. But I knew that the stove kept them warm. The ornate pattern of a grape vine is still clear on the side panel and the deep rust gives it a dimension in our history.

Roots grow inside the bottles. I pull them out gently and take them home. Their labels are faded or sometimes written on the glass. Lightning jars, weird remedies, sarsaparilla, and Moxie. My windowsills are lined with bottles I have found in the holes of abandoned dwellings. I clean out the dirt but leave the imprint of the roots, to remind me where they came from.

I don't know what the ratio is but it seems that for as many old houses that are left standing, there are three that are gone and usually it turns out that these houses have burned to the ground, long ago, erasing themselves from our landscapes, their stories extinguished along with the flames. Other than sheer neglect, there is little else but fire that can kill a house. Houses burned because of faulty woodstoves or dropped lanterns, always horrible mistakes that changed the course of a family's history with their happenstance.

This house has been here since 1762, a history even longer than our nation's. The house is one of the oldest in this town and has come under study for various historical efforts. The Masons lived here first. Then the Willards. Then the Walkers. And now me. Not many for such a long period of our history. A young man who worked on the land here once uncovered a silver buckle in his digging. He polished it and framed it and gave it to Mary and she hung it on the wall of her kitchen. When I bought the farm, he came by and left me a brown bag full of pottery shards, buttons, and glass chips, things he found here, things he felt should come back here.

When I bought the house here at Mary's farm, it appeared strong and straight. And so it was a surprise to find charred wood revealed from behind the old walls. We were gutting the upstairs bedrooms, under the eaves, and discovered that one whole half of the roof had been replaced. When we had all the wallboards removed, the extent of the fire's damage was clear.

The few rafters that had not been replaced were blackened with the soot of that fire. Oddly, one of the men working with us recalled being part of the fire crew that came to the call. "Must have been back in the 1960s," he said, looking up at the newly exposed evidence. "They were lucky they didn't lose the house. Seems to me someone fell asleep, smoking in bed."

At the end of the el, there's a chimney I had hoped to use once I moved in. There was a woodstove attached to it and the first night after I bought the house, I lit it and found the warmth cheerful and hopeful. But soon I was visited by several members of our volunteer fire department.

"Hope you aren't planning to use that chimney," one said to me, in a kind of gruff grumble.

"I already have!" I said, cheerfully.

"I wouldn't keep on with it then," he muttered.

"Why not?" I persisted.

"Well," he said, drawing the word out into several syllables, "I'd say that chimney has had about ten chimney fires, in my memory, at least." As my jaw dropped, he continued his tale: "Yep, I especially remember one New Year's Eve, the guys were so anxious not to have to be interrupted from their party for yet another chimney fire, they sent one of us out here just to babysit the chimney. I call that one condemned and ask you kindly not to use it."

A day later, I pulled the stove and pipe out of the thimble and never used it again.

How many of our old houses escaped near misses like these? How many keep these secrets concealed behind their old walls? I like teasing these stories out from under the eaves. It's different from digging in the old holes because what is here is still with us. But for the quick work of the fire department, perhaps this house would be nothing but an open hole, exposing all that was not worth hauling away. If we had not torn out the walls, maybe I'd never know how close this house came to ending its long reign on the land. I have so little to do with this house's history, except to speak it. What I can say now is that this house has moved into its fourth century and, on the map, it is a small black box, still standing.

THE GARDEN

❧ *Beginnings*

WHEN I FIRST MOVED HERE, there was so much to do, I felt overwhelmed. The big barn, behind the house, was falling. The trees that towered above the house had been heavily damaged by storms, and limbs littered the ground. The house itself would require major work. None of these were things that could be fixed in a day. My mind jumped from one project to the next. I spent the first month here walking about, investigating, measuring, thinking, planning. While I did this, my dogs busied themselves in the grasses and in the brush and when they thought of it, they went down to the pond and took a drink. Because of our close proximity to a busy road, these dogs had spent their lives restrained. Here, they could run free. They scampered here and there, seemingly crazed by all the scents and treasures that had suddenly been put before them. I watched them and their energy felt like my own, a pinwheel of possibilities.

What had always drawn me to this farm were the gardens. Mary was a gardener, by all accounts, a fine one. This was evident in the blooms that ringed the farm all summer long. Lilies bloomed everywhere and her phlox were legendary. On the fence, up by the road, she grew a bright pink rose bush that seemed to bloom even sometimes past the frost.

One year, I can't remember when, a little greenhouse appeared beside her vegetable garden. It was small, free-standing, the kind that you can order out of a catalog. When it was still cold outside, I remember driving by and seeing flowers blooming in there. I envied Mary her little glass house.

Now it was mine. But it had suffered in the meantime. The ice storm of the winter before sent the gnarled limbs of the old apple tree through one side, leaving a big wound, like a hole in a ship. Cold air poured in and it no longer held any warmth.

The last few years of Mary's life, she was ill and her gardening was curtailed. But Mary was a saver and the greenhouse had apparently become a storage place for old flower pots, mostly plastic. By the time I came along, the glass house sheltered only these, the empty beginnings of many a garden past.

The greenhouse was probably the last thing on my list of things that needed to be done but I tackled it first, likely because it seemed possible. I had rented a dumpster, to receive the things from the barn and the house that could not otherwise be used or given away. These plastic flower pots were so old that they disintegrated in my hand. On a hot Saturday morning, I set about to clear space for the beginnings of my own gardens.

As I worked, I wondered, why did she save all these pots? How many did she think she could use? I examined them carefully, wondering if I should save them. I saved the ones made of terra cotta but threw away the rest. By the time I had finished my task, the big green refuse container was full to the brim with the flimsy, feathery containers of an old gardener's dreams.

The glass house thus emptied, I began my repairs. I covered the ice storm hole with plastic and the thermometer on the back wall began to climb. Using a hoe, I dug out the weeds that grew high in the protected warmth. From the local quarry, I brought pickup truck loads of pea stone and wheeled the stone inside with my wheelbarrow.

At the end of that day, my back and my arms ached but, at last, I combed out the final load of stone with my rake. On the shelves, I stacked the few terra cotta pots I had saved. They were still empty, waiting for soil and a handful of seeds. I stepped outside and rolled the glass door shut. Back inside the house, I fixed a late supper, which I ate sitting at the table, facing the wild remains of Mary's last garden and the empty glass house like a bell jar in the midst of it. My dogs came to rest at my feet.

⚘ Rhubarb

THE WORD RHUBARB, when it is used to mean a controversy or dispute, must come from the way rhubarb roots are so twisted and tangled around each other. Though they are a compact, tight ball when you raise them up out of the ground, look closely and you'll see an intricate network of slender red roots pretzeled around each other so tightly that there's almost no way to divide them without breaking them.

The first rhubarb I ever planted came from my neighbor, Archie, who lived across the road. Archie was retired and he spent his time in his garden with his wheelbarrow and his cultivator, a pursuit I envied. One crisp fall day he stopped by and asked if I'd like some of his rhubarb. My garden was in its infancy at that time. "If you don't divide up the roots every few years, they'll choke out," he told me. I was just learning all these things and when I look back I realize he taught me a great deal. "The fall is the best time to transplant the roots," he added.

He made it sound as if I would be doing him a favor, taking a plant or two. I went with him to his garden and watched him separate them. It took strength and gentle persuasion, but he worked it like a brainteasing puzzle and eventually with just the right pressure here and then there, the roots miraculously let go. He showed me how to plant them, which I did, setting the fingers of the red roots pointed-side down in the cool fall soil at the far end of my garden plot, leaving the nubs about an inch above the ground.

In the spring, his rhubarb came up in my garden, little red horns in the still-brown landscape. The stalks were short, less than six inches, but their flavor was sharp and piquant. Every night after supper, I scissored a few stalks into a saucepan, scooped in some sugar, and covered the pot, letting it heat just to a boil. When it was cool, we'd eat it with gingersnaps. If you eat rhubarb every night, it has a cumulative effect on the digestive system. We called it our spring tonic.

There were other rhubarb gifts after that. My father offered me a box filled with roots he'd divided off and I set them in the ground beside Archie's. And my husband brought me some from his mother's garden. I was surprised how different each strain was. The plants from my father were straight and quite red, about eight inches long, an all-around average-Joe kind of rhubarb. My mother-in-law's rhubarb grew the longest stalks I'd ever seen, some of them a yard long, very green and arched, the leaves as big as turkey platters. Surely they could win some kind of ribbon at the fair, if only for their size. All of the rhubarb I have in my garden has come this way, a division of the roots of my friends.

Now when I scissor up the spring tonic, the mixture of the different strains is a nice one, each stalk a distinct reminder of the giver. In the pot, they mingle, surrendering to the heat turned up beneath. Like the roots, they meld together, an inextricable mix of each other. Could we call for a new definition for the word "rhubarb?" Rhubarb: 1. Spring tonic; purge. 2. The inextricable coming together of good things at the right time.

ॐ *The Red Badge of Summer*

IT SEEMS THE LONGER I'M ALIVE the more I feel
that a good tomato is one of the great reasons for living. I like them when they come off the vine with the warmth
of the sun radiating from their perfect red skin. A good tomato
is red in the way that only a ripe tomato can be red, a kind of
red that is sometimes recreated in ceramics but never on paper,
a shade of red that is almost unseen elsewhere in the natural
world, except perhaps in the feathers of tropical birds. A good
ripe tomato stands out in the garden like a flag.

I usually start my tomatoes in March in small cups filled
with earth that is light, as if it's been whipped. I buy this dirt
in bags at the store and, like the tomato's color, the dirt is
unlike any I have ever encountered in the natural world. But it
allows the little white teardrop-shaped seeds to breathe. In the
sunlight of my windowsill, they open quickly and climb out of
the frothy earth. The stalks mature and grow a soft fuzz, like
the cheek of a young boy, with no indication whatsoever of the
tough vines they will become.

In the early part of June, when it's time to put them in the ground, I carry them to the garden on trays, as if I were serving the earth. I dig small holes in the fresh tilled soil. Deep in the bottom of the hole, I plant a lump of chicken manure or hot sheep manure — sometimes I place the corpse of a varmint found by my dog — and then I fill the hole a bit, enough to protect the roots from being burned by the booster but not so much as to lose its edge completely. I take a pot and open it with the blade of my knife. The pot yields easily and I take the root, a swirl of fragile white veins speckled with the powdery potting soil, and hold it in one hand while I pluck all the lower shoots off the stem with the other. Then, holding the fuzzy stem with my thumb and forefinger I position the youngster in the center of the hole, suspending it, while I push the earth in and around the roots. Someone once told me to bury the stem as far as I dare and so I do. It has never done any harm and it seems to keep the stem from becoming spindly and lopsided. Once the plant is square in its hole, I run my hands around the plant making a small hill and then form a kind of moat or collar at the edge of the hill so that water will gather in the resulting trough during the dry season.

I work quickly as I plant each one, a good distance from the next. I've planted tomatoes like this so many times I do it almost without thinking. There's a certain satisfaction that comes with this planting, a rhythm that reminds me of rolling out pie crust or kneading bread dough.

I'm on my knees the whole time, which does not always please me. My knees are not the strongest part of me and I'm often grateful I was not born in a Buddhist monastery where I would have been asked to kneel on cold stone for long periods. I'm happiest on my feet. But, for this task, which comes but once a year, I'm surprisingly comfortable with my knees deep into the warming soil, earth to my elbows, a whisper of gratitude under my breath.

When I'm done, I fetch the watering can and carry water to my charges, filling the moats twice and then stand back to observe the momentary order of these nearly perfect June beginnings, well on their way now to becoming the red badge of summer.

❧ *Looking for Luck*

ONE DAY WHILE WORK was being done on the farmhouse, I came home to find my electrician waiting for me. He was standing in front of my house, staring at the ground. When I called out hello, he looked up, startled as if from a dream.

"Have you lost something?" I asked.

"No," he said, "I'm looking for four-leaf clovers."

"Have you ever found one?" I asked him.

"Oh, sure, I never know when I'm going to spot one so if I've got a bit of time on my hands, I generally look down into the grass."

We both then fell silent and turned our eyes to the ground. No four-leaf clovers were found that afternoon. In fact, although I have lived in clover for a good deal of my lifetime, I've never found a four-leaf clover. This strikes me as odd or unlucky, or both. It isn't as if I haven't looked. At various times, I have devoted time on hands and knees, searching for the lucky cluster. After I moved up here where the fields stretch out from the house like a big cross, I looked even harder. Surely in all this clover, I could find just one.

It doesn't help to know that there are some people out there who find them all the time. I once read about a man in North Adams who claimed he had found "easily" a million four-leaf clovers in his lifetime. In fact, he claims that in a single day he once found 700 lucky clovers. He started finding them when he was four and never stopped. He said that he is, indeed, a lucky man, winning frequently at bingo and Megabucks. Another man once wrote to tell me of his luck in finding four-leaf clovers. He said that he had been finding them "on an average" of one a day. He went on to say that he once gave one to a woman who had trouble getting pregnant. "Yesterday, I received a note announcing the arrival of her baby."

I once wrote about a man named Melvin Longley, a self-taught farmer who lived in Shirley Center, Massachusetts. Melvin, who was an expert on grasses, has since passed away but his son and daughter-in-law, Steve and Mona, continue to live on the family farm, which was recently preserved as a land trust. They invited me to attend the ceremony to dedicate the farm into its new life as a preserve. Before we all went across the road for the ceremonial ribbon cutting at the barn door, Steve surprised me with the gift of a four-leaf clover, pressed between two pieces of waxed paper. I gazed at it in wonder. "Do you find these often?" I asked.

"I find them all the time," Steve said. "I usually walk with my eyes on the ground. They're not so hard to spot."

"Ha! Easy for you to say!" I retorted, and told him wistfully of my fruitless lifelong search.

Irish tradition has it that possessing a four-leaf clover charms the owner with protection. They say that the good luck is even greater if the clover is received as a gift. I took Steve's gift and placed it on my mantel, with fervent hopes for good fortune. At this age, I don't care to get pregnant and, as they say, if you don't play the lottery, you cannot win. My sights are slightly lower in that I'd find it satisfying to be able, at last, to spot the famous shape in the emerging grasses of my rolling fields, which, at this time of year, are green enough to set any Irish eyes to smiling. And, quite possibly, if the right eyes are on them, full of good luck.

ॐ *The Name of the Rose*

WHEN I FIRST BOUGHT Mary's farm, one of the
many natural wonders here was the rose bush that
grew on the post and rail fence out front. The fence alone is a
kind of relic, the rails so old they carry the same lichens seen
on the stones beside the road. Some of the rails have rotted
and I've spent some time shoring these up, as without this
fence, I don't know what would become of this magnificent
rose bush. After I'd lived here a short while, my next neighbor,
Nell Schwartz, stopped by one day to tell me that, many years
ago, she had given this bush to Mary. She told me what kind
of rose it was and allowed that it was very hardy. We stood in
the road then, on that warm June afternoon, and admired the
bush, then decked with the big pink, yellow-centered blooms.
It had grown to perhaps twelve feet in height from the little
stem she had given. We marveled that this rugged bush could
withstand our subzero winters to blaze so brightly in summer.
I did not know it at the time but later learned that Nell was
an expert in roses, nationally known. The day she stopped,
however, I was in the throes of having the house jacked up and

many other changes were taking place here. It was perhaps no wonder that I forgot the name of the rose.

After things began to settle, I realized how spectacular this rose bush really was. It begins to bloom in June, hundreds of hot pink flowers unfolding on the massive bush. Like so much that bursts forth in June, it seems we need to take it in quickly before it goes by. But these roses stay, a month or more, pulsing out their neon message to the occasional car that passes by. The show ends sometime in July but again in early fall, the blossoms return, a repeated exclamation of summer joy.

I kept forgetting to ask Nell to tell me the name again. My plan was that, once I got the house in shape, I would have some spare time and might be able to convince her to spend some time with me. I figured that just a few hours in the garden with Nell would increase my gardening know-how exponentially. And then Nell died, quite suddenly one day in March, when the rose was completely buried beneath the snow. It is when this happens that we experience that sink, the message that says: Take advantage of what you have; tomorrow it might be gone.

So many people had asked me the name of the rose and I had no answer. I asked Nell's husband and her daughters but they did not follow roses as she did. I asked some of her gardening friends but they didn't know either. I felt repentant.

Then one day in June I went on a garden tour. I love to wander through the fanciful creations of other gardeners and see the ways that they arrange their plants, the different varieties of flowers, even trees, that combine to create the easy satisfaction of a summer display. In one garden in the neighboring town of Jaffrey, I came upon a rose bush, one not as big or as old as the one on Mary's gnarled fence, but it was unmistakably the same rose. And the bush was labeled. I felt a thrill that outpaced the fact of the moment: it was just another rose in a well-tended garden. That was all. Knowing the name makes it no less or more beautiful. And yet, somehow, the story is more complete now that I know what Nell told me seven years ago, what I wish I had remembered all along. It is the William Baffin Rose, named for an arctic explorer who ventured into forbidding climates and took root.

❧ The Giant among Us

NOT SO MANY YEARS AGO, I became interested in the phenomenon of growing giant pumpkins, which seemed to gain favor here in the States sometime during the 1980s but which actually began much earlier in the Nova Scotia gardens of a man named Howard Dill, who first developed the seed known as Atlantic Giant, or AG, to those heavy into the fever. At the time, there was speculation by those involved, including the great Howard Dill himself, as to whether or not a pumpkin could be grown to weigh 1,000 pounds. Three and four hundred pounders were popping out of various gardens back then and the very notion of such a large garden vegetable brought forth laughter and amazement.

My attempts were quite ludicrous — the little seedling in its peat pot literally lept off the table onto the floor, and, once planted, the monstrous plant moved across the garden like a Sherman tank on a mission.

I've since learned that the vines of the AG can surge at the rate of two feet a day, the pumpkin itself can expand its girth by six or seven inches a day, and the space needed for such a strange garden is about 1,000 square feet per plant, which is about the size of my entire garden.

You cannot eat these things so why am I growing this, I asked myself and went out and hacked the behemoth vine with a machete, an act of mercy for all the terrified little plants growing in its shadow.

After all, it soon became clear, this was a man's sport, a blood sport that requires heavy equipment and a minimum of twenty men to move the fruit around once it's ready to be taken to the fair. For where else can you find scales capable of weighing such enormity?

They're not even pretty, being a sad, faded color, something like putty. And they are so big they grow in a shape that makes them look exhausted, somewhat flattened and saggy, unlike the perfect round globes we have always known as pumpkins. In fact, a promising looking contender will often collapse, its own weight being too much. Or some explode, like bombs in the patch. Others rot on the bottom, requiring careful attempts to elevate and cushion the beast, like some kind of bedridden invalid. Another very common and "dangerous" aspect of the passage from peat pot to world record is "stem separation," wherein the big guy just rips himself off the life support of the vine. This is serious business, every single one of the growers who indulge in this sport will tell you. They devise intricate, often secret methods of nurturing their quarry, with hypodermic growth injections, intravenous feeds, and earthen cradles. They've long since crossed the sacred threshold of the thousand pounder. Last year, a man in

Henniker, New Hampshire, grew a monster that weighed in at 1,458 pounds. Now some are eyeing the 2,000-thousand pound goal.

It's all about size and so, groping for possible utility, the creative have been known to scoop out the flesh, screw an outboard onto the stern, and set forth on the waterways. Once, a record holder carved his giant into a carriage for his five-year-old daughter to ride in. But most of them just lie there in their exhausted state. A man, also from New Hampshire, has set up a catapult and you can watch him launch these gargantuan vegetables into the air, biggies that vault skyward and then land an acre away with an earthshaking splat, a strangely satisfying sight. Like watching an elephant fly.

For myself, I've taken to growing the little Golden Nuggets, small enough to hold in the cup of my hands and possessing that smooth creamy nutmeg skin, the color of a good pumpkin pie. These are good for pies. And are sweet when carved with a gap-toothed smile and set on the windowsill, a flickering candle within.

❧ *Taming the Wild Bittersweet*

YEARS AGO, WHEN I LIVED down near the Connecticut River, I used to drive by a wild thicket of
bittersweet on my way to work. The vines, like a mass of tangled wires, grew near to the road and, in the early fall, the
undisciplined branches radiated with an abundance of jewel-
like orange and red berries. I wanted so much to stop and
cut some. There is a certain poetry in the way bittersweet sits
in a vase, stretching their curly ends out into the air, as if reaching for something to grasp and twine. The very way it grows
implies a certain longing, a certain quest.

But posted at the edge of the road next to the vines was
a sign that said, simply, No Trespassing. I had seen other, similar signs elsewhere, asking people not to pick the bittersweet.
I hoped that someday, I would have my own patch of bittersweet so that I could cut as much as I wanted and make wreaths
or sprays for my door, as well as arrangements inside, enough
even to give some away. I set the stems, cut when the yellow
pods are just about to open, into a vase without water, which

gives me a colorful and evocative arrangement that will last the entire winter.

That was then. Now I'm here, at Mary's farm, surrounded by, practically strangled by, runaway bittersweet. It's by the fence; it's along the roadside; it's at the edge of the hayfield; it's in my dooryard. When I first came here, I was elated to find all the bittersweet. I had never planted bittersweet, though I had intended to, and yet here it was, all I could ever have dreamed of and more!

But as my time here at the farm increased, my attitude toward this plant changed. The vines took on a kind of insurgency that began to feel frightening. Where once the stone wall contained the vines, now they reached over, gobbling up everything in their path. The stone wall disappeared under the tangled vines. I suddenly became aware that everywhere I looked, the bittersweet vines had encroached or downright taken over.

On a recent fall day, I declared war and went forth with a variety of weapons, including lopping shears, a hand saw, and a machete. Over the summer, I had noticed that there were at least four maple trees whose lives were in jeopardy from the python-like grip of the bittersweet. I was suddenly appalled that I had ever actually thought about planting this ravenous weed, this deadly nightshade. I am pretty sure, in fact, that Mary planted some of this bittersweet. She must have, though certainly much of it had been planted by the innocent droppings of birds. Standing beside a beautiful maple tree, strangulated by the demure bittersweet, I marveled at how innocently we regard anything that is beautiful, how willingly we will invite trouble into our lives if only it will smile at us, and beckon.

Taking my shears in hand, I began to fight the grip of the vine, which was wrapped around the tree in a perfect corkscrew. I felt like the lion tamer, brandishing whip and stool to keep the ferocious animal at bay. I went about like this all day, shearing and hacking, and by the end of the day, I had not only saved the lives of those maples but also liberated several rhododendrons and azaleas, and disentangled a particularly tenacious invader from the thick of my favorite lilac bush. It was a serious day, at the end of which I was exhausted but happy.

I thought back to that beautiful thicket of bittersweet down in Northfield and wondered what naïve notion caused that person to try to protect it with the No Trespassing sign. By now, I'm sure, the vines have devoured not only the sign but the house and the garage as well.

๛ Consider the Lily

CONSIDER THE EASTER LILY, a potted plant with the brief season of a weekend in April. Here in the Northeast they grace our altars, rarely our gardens. Our church has the custom of asking parishioners to order Easter lilies that can be placed on the altar in memory of a loved one. About six weeks before Easter, we can sign up for a lily, or two, and say who it's for. The church charges $10 a lily and we are able to raise a little money this way.

On Easter Sunday, you can smell the lilies as you come up the path, even before you enter the church. The white trumpets fill the altar, the windowsills, and the top of the piano. The pots are wrapped in purple foil and the bright yellow pollen from the center stamens smudges the floor and the white linens like stains of concentrated sunlight. Ours is a small church, and this giving of the lilies is a popular thing that probably contributes to my feeling that, on this day, all the lilies on earth have been brought together into this one place.

Last year Easter was a warm day and there was a good crowd at church. It was a year when I had an abundance of people I wanted to be remembered and so I had ordered four lilies, and once I settled into the pew, I was comforted to see the names of my departed friends printed on the back of the bulletin. Morning light spilled in through the long side windows and I enjoyed seeing my neighbors, who are rarely out of their jeans, dressed in their colorful clothes. The little girls, especially, seemed proud in their frocks, in all the colors of Easter eggs.

And so we rose together and sang and the minister delivered her message, the cheerful news that there is hope after dark hours. This particular service always goes by too fast and, for my taste, it can never provide enough of the happy music. After the last note was played and the words of blessing spoken, I went forward to the lilies and chose four. I clasped them around like a bushel and made my way down the aisle. Others carried lilies too, and so together we undressed the church and brought the fragrance and the sheer whiteness outside, into the sun.

On the lawn we stood and talked, and then I set the pots onto the backseat of my car and started off, my wagon filled with that special Easter scent. I delivered two to friends who had been recently widowed and I kept two. I placed them in my kitchen window and held the aroma there for as long as they bloomed, which in this case was well into May. By that time, it felt safe so I planted them in the east light, beside the back door. People say these plants that come to us in pots from greenhouses in California won't survive outdoors. They say it's not the right climate here in New Hampshire for lilies like these.

In the next couple of months, the leaves on those lilies turned brown at the tips and in general the plants looked poorly. I was too busy to tend them and felt it had probably been foolish to plant them. It wasn't until September that I saw a change. The leaves turned a vigorous green with a distinct sheen. A few weeks later, I walked in through the back door and caught a sweet scent that I at first had trouble identifying. The smell reminded me of another time, something special. I went back outside to see what this was and saw at once the white trumpets, four of them, facing east, broadcasting the fragrance of Easter into the autumn air.

ℬ *The First Storm*

WHAT BETTER STORM IS THERE than a snow-storm, a mighty blizzard? No one (but the perverse) looks forward to a tornado or a hurricane or torrential rains. But, a good, solid northeaster, snow for two days, maybe three? The anticipation for the first real storm of the season is better than Christmas.

Hours before the snow begins, I can smell it, the most peculiar of all odors, more like a sensation than an actual scent. Still, it comes in through the nose, the cold dampness, the gray stillness, the heavy skies, an impending presence, closer and closer. Still in the earth are carrots and parsnips and beets, the last of the potatoes, a whole row of leeks, and the brilliant emerald hedge of parsley. With my basket, I go out across the brown lawn in my black rubber boots. Using my favorite fork, I dig the potatoes, careful not to spear them. I put them in the bottom of the basket and then dig the carrots and the beets, whose greens have withered but which are still hard and a wonderful deep red, almost black. A wind has started and the smell of snow grows stronger. I am planning a stew as I dig, thinking of the warmth inside the kitchen. I pull the leeks and cut the parsley, a small portion of which I will add to the stew but the rest I will snip down and freeze in small bags. I leave the parsnips, to pull in the spring when they will be an extra sweet treat. There it is: the end, my garden a barren stretch of earth, flat but for the wisps of the parsnip tops.

I go to the fence and take down the bird houses. On some dark January day, I will spread newspaper on the kitchen table and sit down beside the stove and paint these little houses, where sparrows and wrens and finches and bluebirds live through the summer months. They are my company in my garden, my cheerleaders. As I work, they swoop above me like the great aerialists that they are, an air show that features not only barrel hoops and figure eights but songs, little cheering songs that seem to be telling me how happy they are that I am there, that we are there together, in the garden.

From the edge of the garden, I carry the big white painted chair into the shed, already stacked high with the winter's wood. The other two chairs go in as well. I take down the clothesline and, using my elbow, I coil it and hang it inside, on a nail beside the garden chairs. Using the wheelbarrow, I bring in all the porch furniture. The table and the couch are too large to carry, so I push them tight against the house wall and cover them with plastic, knowing the snow will drift in during heavy storms.

With good warning and that strong scent to spur me, I work quickly against the track of the storm. When I've done it all, I take one last walk around the yard to see what I have missed. Ah, the bird bath. I bring it in to rest with the chairs for the winter.

It's a big storm coming, they say on the evening news. A green blob marches toward us on the radar screen. They show us scenes of the cityfolk going to the grocery store to stock up on milk and bread, batteries and jugs of water. Everyone seems excited about this first storm, even the reporters who stand at the end of the checkout and ask such questions as, "Are you ready for the storm?" I have filled my lamps with kerosene and new candles are in the candlesticks. Inside my kitchen, I am cutting the beets and potatoes and carrots into chunks and sliding them into the big pot, where cubes of meat have already browned. I've got the flames in the cookstove licking up the stovepipe. The room is warm and instead of snow, I smell herbs and the simmer of sweet meat. I glance outside the window. It is almost dark and I see that the snow has already begun to fall.

FRIENDS

❧ *The Slipshod Reality*

O N N O V E M B E R 18 T H a few years ago, my friend
Floppy turned 100 years old. At least we think she
did. Floppy — short for Florence — lived right down the road
here, in a mythical place known as Tolman Pond, a place of
summer fantasy and winter hardships. Floppy was likely as
beautiful as an old woman as she had once been as a young
woman, though I only met her when she was in her 80s. Even
then, she was distinguished by her sharp blue eyes and her long,
pure white hair, which she wore tied back at her neck with colorful ribbons. She wore slacks and tailored shirts that she made
herself from interesting fabrics. I never saw her in a dress but
she was every bit a lady, raised amidst the uniformed maids and
manicured lawns of Englewood, New Jersey. When she came
to New Hampshire for the summer, she fell in love with a man
named Fran Tolman, who rode horseback with her through the
deep woods of little forgotten places known as Mosquitobush
and Pottersville. She married Fran and became one of the
family. Even though there is an island in the East River off

Manhattan named after her family, once she married Fran, she was a Tolman, dyed in the wool.

Over the years, Floppy had written stories about life on the farm with the Tolman family. "If I ever had a romantic picture of the quaint beauty of rural life, I might have been disillusioned by the slipshod reality," she once wrote. "Perversely, I became attached to it."

Perversely, we all became attached to Floppy, who lived a long time as a widow. Fran died in 1967 and Floppy carried on, living above Tolman Pond in the little house they built in 1930, a handy, practical home that incorporated workshop into living space. She told her stories whenever we came to visit, and she offered her opinion, wanted or not.

Floppy had always greeted the question of her age with a sly smile and a twinkle in her eye. She never revealed it. This invited speculation among those who knew her, especially those who knew her well. One good old friend had actually written to the Vassar alumni office in an effort to solve the puzzle. But some of her family seemed to think they knew how old she was, hence the looming celebration for her century mark.

A few years ago, Floppy had tired of living. She had mentioned to me on a number of occasions that her time was coming and she was getting ready. One dark February day, a few years before she died, she decided it was time and she retired to her bed, saying goodbye to all of us, though not in a dramatic way. She stayed in bed for a couple of weeks until, at last, she emerged, saying that, well, she guessed it wasn't her time, after all. I thought then that she had decided to make it to 100, however long that might take.

When it finally came, on that November afternoon, we all found time to go over and celebrate with Floppy. The family had decorated her house and soft party lights winked at us. We drank punch and ate sweet cakes, all laid out on Floppy's worktable, which had been covered for the occasion with a festive tablecloth. As the party crested, one close relative took me aside and told me he was certain that Floppy was not 100, but 104!

I thought about this for a while, remembering how foxy Floppy had always been on the subject of her age. And remembering the winter when she tried to die but failed. If she was really more than 100, somehow, a few years ago, that big birthday came and went without a party. Now she was having it. She wore that mysterious smile throughout the day, enjoying the memories and the jokes and the gossip (her favorite) that flowed all around her. We all emerged smiling.

Floppy died last winter, a loss we all felt like the loss of a great old tree that's given us shade and protection all our lives. Somehow, we all seemed to think that other folks would come and go but we'd always have Floppy with us, to help us keep the slipshod reality of rural life in perspective. She gave us a great deal, most especially a good reason to want to live to be a hundred. And maybe beyond.

ॐ *Woods Work*

AT THIS TIME OF YEAR, the shadows on the mountain are like deep rivers, running down. I sometimes sit and watch the colors on the mountain change as the light begins to leave us. There is no other time when the mountain looks like this and it's all because of the trees and the brilliant weaving of their heavy, leaf-laden crowns, ready to fall.

There is no time for sitting today. It is the day to cut wood and Henri is coming. Paul and I always did this together, something I greatly enjoyed. He worked the chain saw, which I could not or, rather, would not operate, and I split pieces, using an ax with a long handle that Paul kept painted red so that he could easily spot it on the ground. We often worked in the November woods together and sometimes even in the winter. I have a photograph of Paul, wearing snowshoes and carrying a pack basket on his back. In the basket was our ax, some wedges, a couple of sandwiches, and a Thermos of coffee. I walked behind him with the saw. Friends would sometimes wonder why we persisted with burning wood: so much work, they would say. But to us the wood harvest was as rewarding as any day spent on the slopes.

For the first few years after Paul died, I bought cordwood from a local dealer. He came in a red dump truck and the logs slid out of the bed with an earth-shaking clatter. All I had to do was stack it and carry it to the stove. But I missed the ritual of our woods work. My first winter here at Mary's farm was marred by the hiss of wet wood, mostly because I had not had the time to get the wood in, but also because I was alone.

Behind the barn was a pile of tree-length logs, left here by Mary, or perhaps her son-in-law. The logs were twenty or thirty feet long and stacked high, like a Connecticut River logjam. One day when Henri was here doing other work, he suggested that he could work these logs into firewood for me. "Only if I can help," I said.

Henri likes to work. A slender man with a beaked nose and a woodsman's beard, he moves quickly through a task and leaves little time before he starts another. Motion seems to be his best friend. In recent years, he has helped me cheerfully with many jobs.

I've hardly gotten the breakfast dishes into the drainer before I hear his truck pull into the yard. He backs the trailer with all his equipment up to the barn, tight to the log pile. I join him, and we set up a work site with the splitter within reaching distance of the log pile and the truck backed up to the splitter. We don't want any steps in between, just pivoting motions.

With his chain saw, Henri cuts big pieces from the logs and piles them next to the splitter. They are big and round, like barrels. I take the ones I can heft and set them onto the bed of the splitter. It's a hydraulic system; when I push the lever down, the wedge creeps forward and drives itself into the wood, opening it and exposing the smooth red grain of the oak. Some of the big pieces require me to pass them through the splitter six or seven times before I get the right size pieces for my stoves. I throw the split lengths into the back of the truck, which causes a particular clatter, wood on metal.

It's a lot of noise, the whine of Henri's saw and the growl of the splitter, which revs appreciably, as if it were clearing its throat, when the wedge hits the wood. If we need to talk, we use hand signals. The wood is mostly oak, and its sweet musky scent fills the air.

With a quick lunch eaten on the tailgate, the day passes. At the end of the day, we have stashed several cords in the shed. We once again silence the engines and Henri turns and looks at the mountain. He loves the mountain, feels its power and beauty in each season. "Look at that!" he says.

The colors, swirled in orange and red and yellow, are a great flame, lit by the angle of the sun. It's been a good day, a great day, warmed by the fire on the mountain and the promise of good, dry wood throughout the winter.

❧ *November's Walls*

IN NOVEMBER, THE FOLIAGE dies back and we can see our stone walls again. We take them for granted here, these lines of stone, magically adhered by nothing other than their weight and the peculiar fit of their jagged edges. "Something there is that doesn't love a stone wall," Robert Frost opined but, really, I think there is something that *does* love a stone wall, something that has kept them here, a century or two after they've been laid. These walls stay up, for the most part, in ways that defy logic. Last year I visited with a farmer in Vermont who pointed to the wall behind his house and told me it had been built during the Revolutionary War. It looked freshly laid. There are the famous walls here, the arch bridges and the great walls, wide and flat as a road, on which a wagon and a pair of horses could be driven. The walls at my house, though, are common, unremarkable and yet, to me, they are special.

I have a number of walls, as does anyone who has fields. The walls in my fields are kind of unloved, if that is what Frost meant by walls that have fallen down. Some of them just end in the middle, connecting nothing, as if they had no function but to hold the rocks that the farmer hauled out of the fields with his stone boat.

I have one wall, though, that I admire often. This wall between the road and the hayfield has a purpose, like a fence or a boundary. It's different from the walls in my field. The stones, some of them anyway, seem cut or quarried and are of a different granite from the stones around here. And the wall is laid just a little bit more deliberately, just a little bit more artistically. Some of the stones are very large and the smaller stones arch over the big ones like beads on a frame. Since my screen porch faces this wall, I find myself studying it, quite often, the way I might study a sculpture or a painting. My eye rests on the surface of the stone and then on the chinks, a perfectly balanced creation with openings just right for chipmunks and other small creatures that I sometimes spy ducking in and out between the stones.

In spite of this one, splendid wall, I wasn't happy with the walls that I had. Most of them were scattered and uneven. I wanted a garden wall, one in front of which I could plant lilies and hollyhocks, foxglove and iris. I called the local stone mason and he came, a big, dark, handsome man of Mexican descent. He tore apart the crumbling wall that had been there and dug down into the earth for the footing and started building anew, the stones piled beside him in a primitive heap. He took this one, and then that one and turned them over to find the right side. He fitted and tested and discarded the ones that wouldn't do. He took stones from the old fallen down walls in the field and brought them to the job and examined their surfaces. He liked their "patina" — the deep gray and the netting of lichen. He worked for several days on his mosaic. From inside the house, I could hear his work, the solid *thunk* of stone hitting stone, the tap of the masonry hammer, the leverage of the crowbars. He worked shirtless in the hot sun and it made me think of ancient things like Egyptian pyramids and the Great Wall of China. To make his wall, the old farmer or whoever it was who built the wall by the field used the same techniques that the Egyptians and the Chinese had. My stone mason used a tractor with a bucket loader to retrieve the stones but, when it came to laying one stone on top of the other, he used his bare hands and just a few tools, a hammer and a bar and, mostly, his eyes, to create the symmetry we so prize in these structures.

He was done in a week, for him, another wall to add to his life's work, for me, a magnificent new backdrop for my flowers, which would rise and bloom, come spring. I wonder who will come, in the centuries that follow, and study the lines and the chinks and the swell of the boulders and try to understand who made this wall. And why.

✌ *Thanksgiving on the Range*

ONE OF MY MOST CHERISHED belongings is my Glenwood wood cookstove. I have had this stove for most of my adult life, coming into it during my first marriage and bringing it into my second, with the same determination one might bring one's child or beloved dog. Love me, love my stove. But that wasn't necessary, for Paul loved the stove as much, perhaps more than I did. The stove was made at a time when both form and function sat equally on the scales. The smooth black curves of her legs and warming shelf are sufficient for those who are drawn to beauty alone. The complicated mechanisms of the slide drafts, combined with the airflow around the oven box, are what fascinate the engineers. The plump sweet loaves of Anadama bread that emerge from her toasty oven are enough to sway anyone in between.

In summer, the stove sits silent, occasionally adorned with a vase of apple blossoms or peonies. When friends gather, I sometimes dress the stove with a colorful cloth and laden her with the blessings of the potluck. My other Glenwood, a big old gas range, does the work. But in November, Black Beauty comes back to life, and we enjoy a grateful reunion of warmth and utility.

Because I'm so used to this stove, it always surprises me that the stove's very being does not explain itself. "What is this?" a visitor may ask, giving the stove a quizzical look. "Do you use this?" others politely inquire.

A few years ago, I was in residence at the MacDowell Colony, a retreat for artists and writers. I was unique among the other residents, as I lived nearby. Most came from faraway parts of the United States and even Europe. Many came from New York City. I happened to be at MacDowell at a time that included the Thanksgiving holiday so I invited my new friends to join me at my home for a turkey dinner. Early on Thanksgiving day, we made the journey to my house, laden with grocery bags filled with the ingredients for a home-cooked turkey dinner. My artist friends, who until that moment I knew only as absorbed writers, composers, and painters of canvas, came to in the kitchen like mummies from their tombs. Paul, who I knew as a composer of bombastic phrases, went to work on the gravy. David, a gifted cartoonist, made bread. Rhoda, a novelist, appointed herself chief cook and oversaw the rest.

What amazed and fascinated them was the stove. "You can actually roast a turkey in there?" they asked, somewhat anxiously, needing to know that this plan for a great meal was not going to fail them due to a weird and antiquated stove.

"Yes," I assured them as I fed split lengths of oak into the firebox, hardly able to wait to be able to show off the deep brown enamel of the turkey's roasted sides when it would emerge from the oven in a few short hours. Somewhat dramatically, I showed off the stove's foot pedal, an invention long since abandoned, though I never can figure out why. Both hands full with the roasting pan, I tapped the pedal with my toe. *Voilà!* The oven door swung open and I safely nudged the bird into the warm chamber, closing the door as if to a magic box. On top, the lids of pots tapped as onions boiled and cranberries simmered. The room filled with the indescribable scents of a holiday at home.

I still get notes from my friends, remembering their amazing dinner cooked on a woodfired stove. I think of them in their city apartments, which is where most of them reside, and wonder if they think of me as a pioneer cook. I don't but neither do I think of my stove as anything but the way it should be.

ॐ *December Babies*

Those of us who were born in December often come late, or so say the old wives, claiming that these fiery infants aren't anxious to come forth into the cold world. I was apparently not interested in that cold entry, as I was born on December 10th rather than on November 14th, the day my mother expected me. That was also the day that Queen Elizabeth gave birth to Prince Charles. I don't think my mother ever quite got over the disappointment that I didn't come when I was supposed to, as I think she liked the idea of giving birth on the same day as the queen.

A number of years ago — actually thirty, to be exact — one of my closest friends was expecting her first baby. She and her husband had chosen to live in the woods, with only a horse for transportation. They lived like pioneers in a cabin they had built themselves, a shelter with no electricity or telephone, almost three-quarters of a mile from the road. Her due date was early December and I was not the only one who worried that she might not make it out of the woods in time. Would she ride her horse to the hospital, we wondered. Maybe she wondered, too, as the due date came and went and no baby arrived. At last, she went into the hospital, where labor was induced and she gave birth to a beautiful, rugged little boy, two days after Christmas. The boy is now a man, six feet and more.

If nothing else, December babies have stories to tell.

But the most astonishing birth story that I know of was not about being born late, but about being born too soon. This happened to a friend who was born two months early, into the chill month of December, in the 1930s, in the hills of Vermont.

It was nearly Christmas and the night that she was born there happened to have been a great snowstorm which blocked the roads and especially the high hill where her family farmed. Fortunately, the family doctor lived on the same hill so he was able to get to the house just before the little girl emerged, small as a bird, very likely too small to survive.

These were the instructions the doctor gave to her father: fill a half a dozen Mason jars with boiling water and place them around the sides of a wooden box. Wrap the baby in a woolen blanket and place her into the jar-warmed box. Set the box into the oven and leave the door open. Then go upstairs and start the stove in the bedroom. Keep the door to the room shut and raise the temperature to ninety-eight or ninety-nine, as high as you can get it.

Her father carefully followed the doctor's plan, tightly sealing the room and kindling a roaring fire with thin, split sticks. He kept his tiny daughter in the oven until the bedroom was ready, at which time he carried her up to the hot room and left her in the cradle.

When he returned, he saw, to his horror, that she had turned blue. A quick-thinking farmer, he knew in an instant what she needed. Throwing open the window, he held the gasping infant out into the December night, where she gulped in the icy air, the balm that she needed.

My friend is healthy and every bit as rugged as those of us who slept through their due date. She's in her sixties now, a good age to reflect on such a fearsome entry into this unprotected life, which she sometimes does while sitting out on the grass of her father's farm. Her father is gone now but she keeps his farm as a summer retreat. It is much as he kept it, minus the animals, and that room where he created her incubator is largely unchanged.

I love her story because it reminds me that, though life is fragile and it is often taken from us in ways that leave us mystified, still, a box of warm Mason jars, a woodstove, and the cold air of a December night were, at one time, all that was needed to save a tiny life.

ॐ *The Afterlife*

WHEN MY HUSBAND Paul died, he left among his things a small treasure. Paul had many keepsakes: his high school ring, his favorite set of chisels, his old Farmall tractor. But this one was different: a small Egyptian figure that he found when he was a little boy, buried in the dirt beside his family's garage. He kept this mysterious figure in a worn oblong box that once contained a brand new pair of pliers. He had shown this mysterious object to me when I first knew him and we both puzzled over the little figure, which looked perfectly authentic, carved from some kind of greenish stone, with a Sphinx-like headdress and hieroglyphs inscribed like a skirt. But we knew nothing about such things and knew no one who could tell us. We thought it might have been a toy, or a replica. As it was, it could either lie like a corpse, arms folded across the chest, or stand like a sentry. In all, the little man could fit in the grasp of one hand. The biggest question for us was: how did this ancient object come to rest in a backyard in Northfield, Massachusetts, where some items barely more than 100 years old are often considered valuable and rare?

After Paul died, I put all his treasures into a blanket box. But the Egyptian figure, I kept in a cubbyhole of my desk. Perhaps, I thought, one day I could find someone who might know something about these things, enough at least to be able to tell me if it was real.

The answer to that question lay right down the road here, in the head of a woman named Diana Larkin, whom I knew as a neighbor before I knew as an Egyptologist. How often does one stumble across someone like this? Probably as often as one stumbles across an Egyptian figurine buried in one's backyard. One summer day, I brought the stone figure out from his resting place and showed him to Diana. She took him in her hand and said, without hesitation, "Oh, yes, this is very real. I have catalogued many of these at the museum at Mount Holyoke." And she offered to do some research for me.

A few weeks later, Diana presented me with her report. Given in a scholarly fashion, it answered most of the questions that we had. Possibly dating from 600 B.C., the figure was known as a *shabti*. These figures, placed in tombs, represented individuals who could be called upon to do manual labor in the afterlife, relieving the deceased from such a prospect. According to Diana, the figurine that Paul had found so many years ago had once been placed in the tomb of a man named Imhotep (which means "Come in peace" or "Welcome"). Imhotep, she explained, was just an ordinary man, not a king or prince. The figure was molded from a clay-like substance called faience, common in ancient Egypt. His tiny worn arms were crossed over his chest. He held a hoe in one hand and a seed bag in the other, which indicated his readiness to work in the fields for Imhotep, should the need present itself. Diana translated the hieroglyphic text that encircles him. It ends with the statement, *"Here I am," you shall say.*

Apparently, even in ancient times, *shabtis* were found far beyond Egypt. Some have been excavated in several countries bordering the Mediterranean. But Massachusetts? Diana tells me that travelers to Egypt, especially in the early part of the 20th century, bought *shabtis* as souvenirs. So it is conceivable that someone in Northfield came home with such a figurine. And the rest of its journey can and will remain a mystery. For the time being, I've brought the little fellow out of his box and stood him up on the bookcase in the living room, a reminder of the long arm of history, how it can reach almost 3,000 years and halfway around the world, completely by accident. "Here I am," he says to me, and I smile at his readiness to help.

✣ Auction Magic

FOR A NUMBER OF YEARS, I've been fascinated by auctions, or auctioneers. We have a small population of them in this area and I frequent them, at once to purchase bargains, like the complete set of good wicker porch furniture I once picked up for $12, but also to be entertained and to be invited to imagine.

My house is virtually furnished with auction finds, each piece carrying with it a story. I especially like estate auctions, held on the grounds of the homes being liquidated. Being there, watching the items carried from the house, held up for inspection and sold in a trice, adds color to their essence. We all gather, like viewers at a wake, paying respects to the objects that so clearly represent the passing of an era. We put them together into an imagined life: the dirt-crusted farm tools delineate a hard life of hand work; the red-handled cooking implements evoke a cinnamon-scented kitchen; the rocking chair with wear on the seat and on the head rest suggests many evenings of gentle comfort.

I especially like the Saturday night auctions at Fred's. Fred, round and red-cheeked, has spent a lifetime emptying old houses and appraising objects. He is knowledgeable and shrewd. His auctions are a mix of items from various sources. But he sometimes gives us a glimpse into their history. Recently, he held up a pair of binoculars for sale. I had inspected them before the sale. They were of good quality and I had a notion to bid on them. He started the sale, "Who'll give me $50 for this fine pair?" and then he lowered them, pausing in his pitch, and spoke more casually into his microphone. "You know," he said, "every time I go into one of these houses where the old lady has died, what is the first thing I see when I walk in the front door? There on the pine stand by the front window, are the binoculars. Every single time. And, you know, these ladies are not birdwatching!" And in that aside, Fred gave us not only the vision of our elders watching over us and their town, but also a glimpse into his own world, a constant appraisal not only of objects but of lives lived.

On Saturday afternoons, the auction hall is fragrant with chili and meatloaf, for sale at the concession stand. The back of the hall is crowded with Windsor chairs, harvest tables, pine cabinets, blanket chests, and jardinières. The shelves are lined with syrup buckets, redware, silver plate, wristwatches, and old metal toys. The walls are often hung with paintings and Oriental rugs. Sometimes on the sides are such things as a canoe or a kayak, and once or twice, a railroad freight cart, all ready for new life. We, sanctioned snoops, mill about, squeezing around the tight lines of furniture, opening lids, upturning plates and crocks, examining rims, and looking for hidden labels or dates. We test the chairs for comfort, open the doors of the hutches, and bring out the drawers to inspect the undersides and the joints. We squint. We rub. We crouch on hands and knees.

The sale begins at 6, sharp. Fred mounts the podium, which is made of pine and adorned with one sign that admonishes: No Opium Smoking. Up there, he has the vantage of a cleric. He holds us with his words. The runners line up promptly and one by one the items are held aloft, while Fred performs his magic. Most offerings take no more than a minute or two to gain their price. Within two hours, the vanishing act of the auction is complete: the hall is empty, the shelves and walls bare. And we collect our purchases, load them into our trucks, and convey them into our lives, still unfolding.

ஜ் *Adrift*

IN THE WINTER, MY HEROES are the men who drive the snowplows up this hill. Because the farm here is high (probably 2,000 ft. el.), there is usually more snow here than there is even in the village, which is just a mile away but most of that mile is downhill. So, if there is a foot of snow in the village, there's a foot and a half here. I sometimes wonder how my predecessors managed in the days before heavy equipment. I know that they had huge snow rollers, driven by teams of four and sometimes six horses. These rollers were used on the main roads but I doubt that these rollers ever came up here to the farm.

One winter, in a good northeaster, the snow started falling in the afternoon and accumulated with such speed, it seemed I could see it climb up against the windowpane, an inch at a time. The snow rose as if it were being shaken from a sifter and by midnight, the landscape in front of the house looked like a white desert. It is when I see this great expanse of unbroken snow that I feel that direct kinship with those who came before me. I think of dark, lonely, and cold nights when any thought of leaving the homestead would have been absurd. The power was out. No plow came. I felt a kind of electric excitement which is probably part fear and part wonder, the feeling that I haven't moved an inch and yet everything around me has profoundly changed.

When the wind gets to a certain speed up here, it has a distinctive voice, which breathes, high and then low and then silent for a breath and then back to a scream. The wind worked its voice and somewhere, every now and then, in the barn or maybe on the house, a loose door or shutter banged. The snow drove against the windowpanes with a grainy sound, like wind-driven sand. I lay sleepless through the long night, feeling adrift on a huge ocean of snow. Toward dawn, I heard an engine, very mute at first. Using my thumb lamp to light my way, I went to the east window and in the distance I could see a dim light. What else could it be but the plow? In big storms, the crew does not use the standard dump truck and plow but instead they use the grader, which in the summer is used to iron the washboards out of the dirt roads.

Like two wide eyeballs, the brilliant spotlight-style headlights of the grader pointed up the road. They illuminated the storm, which was driving into them at a slant. In front of the blade, there was nothing but a flat, featureless expanse of new snow. The big machine toiled up the hill, an inch at a time. I can only imagine the weight of the snow behind that big shiny blade. Closer and closer it came. There are no markers on this road, except perhaps the periodic telephone pole. It's usually Wes who drives the grader and I don't know how he could see where he was going into that wilderness. As he reached the house, I could all but hear the straining of the big machine as it groaned against the enormous load of the snow. The big tractor wheels turned slowly and tentatively as the blade pushed the snow to the side and left behind a clear path. In a matter of ten or twenty minutes, the road was cleared. When the sun had risen, everything seemed clear and simple again. Brian, who plows my driveway, came to liberate me. With the sun strong against the new snow, I backed my car out of the garage and drove into town, suddenly so free.

❧ Winter Boarders

I SUPPOSE I AM NOT the first widow who has taken to renting out a room in order to make ends meet. For a widow, a spare room is like the hay off the field or corn in rows. It is a cash crop, profitable if well managed.

Once, I swapped room and board to a man, a friend of a friend. In exchange for the meals and the room, he spent the summer painting my house. He was happy, and so was I. That time, it worked.

Another time, I rented a room to a man who taught at a university in the south. He wanted to experience working at a magazine and so he came to Dublin for the summer. He inquired about my spare bedroom and we agreed upon a fee. But when he arrived, he unloaded so much out of his car, I feared he was here for the duration. Other quirks emerged and within three days, I had to ask him to leave. I won't go so far as to say he frightened me. But, a little. An example of nipping something in the bud, is all I need say.

It's odd because, offhand, I don't recall having rented a room very often but when I start thinking back over the years, there are many examples that come to mind and most of them cause me to puzzle over why each encounter seems odd and perhaps ill advised when viewed in the perspective of time. I once visited Thomas Wolfe's home in Asheville, North Carolina. His mother ran a rooming house there and he grew up in that environment. As I walked through the rooms of that big house, I realized how he was able to harvest stories from the people who came and went. And why: people who come and go are not living normal, quiet lives. Something has spurred them out of their marriages or out of their jobs and they have set forth on a quest of sorts, which leaves them in need of a place to sleep. At least for a while.

Most recently, a man came to me last fall and inquired about renting. He was in the midst of a divorce and needed a place just for the cold months as he had a place to live on a lake in the summertime. He was charming and pleasant, and in spite of all my other encounters, I reasoned that there would be no harm in taking him in for the winter. And so he came, full of surprises. He brought with him not only his dog, but a reptile in an aquarium and white lab rats in a cage. He brought also his own easy chair and a big TV and VCR and settled in for the long winter. I had not really expected any of this, nor had I expected the complications of his life, which followed him in like snowy footprints. He did not mean harm and he did not cause any. But his life was large, with many characters and many chapters. Last winter was colder than average, and so there was even more reason to welcome the spring, as he packed and left.

They all leave, most of them in the same way, a cautious goodbye and both of us wishing the other good luck. Long ago, when I first rented a room to a stranger, I thought of it as risky and temporary, something to fill in for the time being. Now I realize this is part of my life and the men who have come and gone are parts of my family, in that odd way of Thomas Wolfe's mother's boarders. They all have their stories and for a while, I become part of theirs as they become part of mine.

❧ To Save a Sheep

For a number of years, it was my pleasure to host a flock of sheep that belonged to my neighbor, David. When the grass was high, David and his dogs would herd the sheep down the road from his farm, a mile or so up the road, and corral them through my gate into the waiting green field. He usually brought thirty or forty at a time. If I did not see them coming down the road, I could hear them. The peculiar pattern of their small running hooves on packed pavement had a distinctive sound, a muted stomp, like a thousand fingertips drumming.

I always felt I got the best of both worlds in this deal: David and his shepherds took care of any and all of the needs of these big wooly beasts while they kept my field trim and at the same time provided me with a moving picture out the window. My one task, perhaps, was to keep watch.

One day, as evening was falling, I was getting ready to go out with a friend. We were about to get into the car when we glanced into the field. At the far end, we saw what looked like a sheep on its back, feet in the air. We sprinted into the field.

It was a big sheep, indeed on her back, not dead but breathing heavily. This ewe was huge, easily 200 pounds or more and her stomach bulged out like a woman in late term. "She's trying to give birth!" I cried to my friend, who knew even less about animal husbandry than I did. I had no idea what was wrong with this sheep but than seemed like a good guess. We knelt beside the panting animal and stroked her belly. "Breathe!" I said. "Push!"

After a few short minutes we realized we needed help. I jogged back to the house and called David, who was not home. I called several of his shepherds but no one was home! I thought of a neighbor, an older gentleman who keeps goats and bees and seems to know what all of the rest of this world has forgotten about animals and the natural world in general. He answered on the ninth ring. I blurted out our problem. He let a few seconds pass before he said, "Yup." I asked him if he could come down and he again allowed some tension to build before he said, "Yup."

I went back out into the field and continued the vigil beside this dying sheep. By now, her stomach was grotesquely bloated, her breathing short gasps. After what seemed like hours, Dick's little red pickup truck rolled slowly into the driveway. He parked and got out, and, with all the deliberation of a lawyer approaching the bench, he crossed the field to where I and my anxious friend knelt.

Dick stood for a long moment with his arms crossed, assessing the situation. All of our theories about this being a failing pregnancy seemed to pass by him. At last, he stepped toward our distressed mother-to-be, took hold of her two front hooves and, with a practiced flick of his wrists, he whirled this enormous creature into the air. She landed on all fours and ran off like any frightened animal would.

We looked in amazement at Dick. He turned to us and said, slowly, "Sometimes they fall and they can't get up."

I thought he was joking. Surely this was more than just a case of a fallen ewe. You mean she was not about to give birth? You mean she was not dying of some dread disease? No, he explained. If they somehow get onto their backs and can't right themselves, gas builds up in the stomach and they can die from the pressure. "You just need to get them back up and they'll be fine," he said. "She would have been dead by morning."

There was a time when just about any one of my neighbors would have known exactly what to do for this sheep. I wished for just a single volume of Dick's library of knowledge, much of which had come to him from all the considerable days he had spent tending his animals. That was just one day in my education and I was relieved to know that next time, I would know how to save a sheep.

ॐ *The Coyote*

I AM SURROUNDED BY COYOTES HERE. I hear
them in all seasons, but more frequently in summer,
when our windows are open. Most often, the haunting cries
come at night, a yodeling howl and then a chanting chorus that
goes round and round like a fugue. I am often awakened by
this revelry in the middle of the night, and so are my neighbors. We talk about these incidents as we would about a storm:
Did you hear them last night? we ask each other when we meet.
Wasn't it something?

Last summer, on a brilliant sunny afternoon, I heard
them, carousing over the ridge and I stopped still and listened.
I felt a tide of fear rise in my veins. I asked the game warden
if I should worry about my dog. Mayday is a little schnauzer,
no more than twenty pounds and built like a pork roast. I fear
she might be tempting to these ranging wild dogs as they sweep
across the fields, searching for prey. The warden said, "Well,
maybe. A little bigger and I wouldn't worry but she's just at
that marginal size. Coyotes (he pronounced it Ky-oats) are
opportunistic: They won't come looking for her, but if she's in

their path, and they happen to be hungry, well, they might just take her." He advised that I might want to get a bigger dog, as a companion for Mayday.

I filed that information. Mayday likes to sniff in the fields and I don't want to keep her from that pleasure. But she's alone up here, the single domesticated animal in a big place where I've seen bear, moose, fox. It's common for me to open my eyes in the morning and, before I've lifted my head from the pillow, spy out the window a big buck, grazing in the field.

Coyotes are fearless. I know of a man who lives in the next town, a quaint village with a lot of pretty white houses all in a row. His house has a big front porch, looking out on the main street. He says that one day he looked out onto his porch and there on the step was a coyote, sitting on its haunches like a dog. The man went out to try to shoo the animal away and the coyote just turned and looked at him and didn't budge. Not even an inch.

Like the deer, I've seen the coyotes crossing the field. They are big, like mutts, with high hind legs and a bushy, fox-like tail. I pretty much know where they live, down in the hollow in the back of the big field across the road. I don't take Mayday down there on our walks.

One morning, I was sitting near the window, reaching to dial the phone. Mayday was on the couch on the porch, as is her custom. She likes to keep an eye on things from that perch. Of a sudden, she leapt down, barking furiously. This can often mean a chipmunk so I didn't feel any sense of alarm but out of the corner of my eye I saw what I thought was a dog run by. It had a reddish coat and a big bushy tail. Coyote! I lurched from my chair and ran, yelling, *Mayday! Mayday! Come!* Mayday was already into the field and by the time I caught up with them, the coyote had stopped, dead, and was silently staring at Mayday, whose bark was shrill and insistent. I was shouting fruitlessly at the top of my lungs — *Git! Git! Go home you coyote you!* — and Mayday was moving closer to the big dog. His coat was glistening in the bright morning sun and a breeze gently raised his fur. His staring eyes were two black holes. He was like a statue, staring back, unperturbed by this scene. Mayday was within ten feet. I was parallel with her, matching her bark with my yell.

Suddenly, I stopped. And Mayday stopped. The three of us stood in our triangle, silent, trapped in our stare. I moved sideways toward Mayday and caught her collar, swept her up into my arms and slowly backed away. The coyote stared intensely at the two of us, a woman and her dog, a united front, and I thought for a moment that what flashed from his eyes was not hunger — but envy.

ఞ *Cousin Frank*

COUSIN FRANK LIKES TO HUNT for treasure in my fields. Frank is not really my cousin. He is my first husband's cousin and he was the best man at our wedding. Frank and his cousin, my ex-husband, have each had several wives since that long ago time of our wedding. Right now, Frank is "still looking," as he says.

Frank grew up in the Bronx so he says certain words rather distinctively — for bird, he says boid and for toilet, he says terlet. For a long time, he worked for the phone company, doing circuit work, and when he had some down time at work, he used to call us up from where he lived in New York and ask us if we wanted to call anyone — anywhere on earth. We could usually think of someone so we'd talk for free and laugh about it afterwards. Sometimes he would come to see us in New Hampshire but he was always restless and he never stayed long.

He's retired now, even though he's not quite sixty, and he lives part of the time in Florida. What he does now, apparently almost all the time, is look for lost things. He uses a metal detector, which looks like a flattened Saturn with its ring, on the end of a long cane. With headphones, he can hear when the wand passes over something metallic. Since he started looking, he has found an astonishing number of things, including coins of all kinds and vintage, a Revolutionary War medal, and an 18K diamond ring. In fact, he has several cases of rings that he has found on beaches and at public places. His favorite place to look for things is Miami Beach at low tide.

He has so many gold rings stashed in the velvet slots of these cases that when he lifts the lid, he seems suddenly like a pawn jeweler, opening shop. He has favorites and will tell you the value of some of them but he says he has never sold anything he's found and does not intend to. "I just like to find things," he says. "And keep them."

He was brown as old leather when he showed up at my door last spring, having just come back from Florida. "Would you mind if I did a little looking?" he asked me. That time, he found a button he said was from the Civil War and a metal clasp. The clasp was rusted and caked with earth hard as clay. I wondered how he knew it was anything but a clot of dirt. I also took his word about the button.

For the hunt, he wears a fanny pack around his waist — for a place to carry the things he finds — ties his pantlegs with rubber bands and slings the metal detector over his shoulder. In his left hand, he carries a shovel. When he's out in the field, he swings the big wand in an arc with the grace of an athlete. He could be casting seed on the hayfields, the way he moves. It looks a little bit like he's testing the earth, listening deep. Every once in a while, he stops, puts his hand to his earphones, and steadies the detector over a small area. Then he pushes the shovel in with his foot and lifts a hunk of sod. Leaning down, he rummages for the source. He brings it up close to his face, studies it, and either puts it back or stashes it in his pouch.

This spring, Frank came again, as soon as the snow melted. He was looking happy. He had a pretty woman with him. She was as tanned as he was and they were both wearing sunglasses. "This is Mary," he said. "I found her in Florida."

She had her own metal detector and together they went out into my field, searching.

Frank hasn't ever found any gold rings in my field. This time he unearthed an old pocket knife, probably from the 1950s, and a copper, dome-shaped object that he said was the bell from an old telephone, the kind you cranked up like on Lassie. Before they left, he gave both these things to me and I put them on the shelf alongside the button and the clasp.

Mary, apparently, was not a keeper. I heard Frank is back in Florida, by himself, looking for treasure.

ॐ The Hot Noise of Summer

MY GRANDFATHER'S HOUSE had a sleeping porch, which, so far as I could tell, was his favorite room in the whole house. Beneath it was the sunporch, which ran a close second. But the sleeping porch had an almost mystical feel to it, part of which was that it was high up, next to the treetops. My grandfather (never my grandmother) loved the hot nights when he could sleep out there. The sleeping porch was a big room, open on three sides, with several daybeds, all of them covered in Indian print spreads. Screening covered the big window openings and, for privacy, there were bamboo shades that rolled down but which still allowed air to pass through.

I was very young, not even ten, but I remember the nights sleeping out there with my grandfather. I sometimes spent the weekend at my grandparents' and we usually played cards before bedtime. For this, my grandparents had a wicker table and some chairs out on the porch. My grandmother carried orange juice and pecan cookies upstairs on a tray and we played hearts through the heat of the night. In between turns, my grandmother leaned back in her chair. She held her cards in a fan. She would touch the tip of each card with her finger and then, once sure of her hand, she used the fan to cool herself. Outside, the crescendo of the cicadas faded in and out as if to dramatize the heat's energy while the katydids countered with their short, scratchy reply.

After we folded the last hand, my grandfather settled into the bed beside the west window and my sister and I climbed into the beds to the north. My grandmother kissed us goodnight and told us to remember to try to lie really still which would keep us cooler than if we tossed about in frustration. Then she disappeared into the bedroom which adjoined the porch.

"Think of ice floating on a river," my grandfather always said, just before falling into a snore.

I don't remember any hot nights here in New Hampshire to equal those hot nights in New Jersey. Up here on the hill, there is almost always a breeze and there are no cicadas or even katydids. But we do have heat. Intense heat wicks my energy and I sometimes find myself sitting in a lawn chair, drinking iced tea when I ought to be doing something more energetic. I often wonder how anything gets done in southern climates. Which is why I live where I do. Twenty below zero never gets in my way so much as a hot, humid ninety-five degrees.

I hope it goes without saying that I do not have air conditioning in my house. Open windows and a good fan are all that I need to make myself comfortable. But during hot spells, the urge to sleep outside still comes over me. I have a small open porch, which has screening from top to bottom. It's big enough for a few chairs and a table. In the corner, I've pushed an old daybed against the screens. On really hot nights, I sometimes take my pillow out onto the porch and settle onto the couch. Lying there in the still heat, I can hear night hawks and owls. Sometimes, I hear animals crashing about in the thicket. As I drift off to sleep, I pretend I'm a block of ice, floating on a river. What I miss, though, is the hot noise of the cicadas and the gentle snoring of my grandfather.

❧ Struck Gold

O N ONE OF THE RARE SUNNY DAYS late last
summer, I took an old milk jug off its peg and
walked out into the back field where I know there is a nice
tangle of blackberry bushes. Throughout the summer, the hay
grows tall and walls off the fields. In August, the hay is cut and
baled and then I can go back out into my wide open spaces.

At the outer edge of the field, I found that the berries
had grown plump and dark, perfect picking. The birds had not
gotten them all yet. I nabbed one and popped it into my
mouth. The deep purple fruit was warm and soft and my
tongue broke it easily, making it all sweet juice. Like a hungry
traveler, I plucked another one quickly, and another, tossing
them back like little candies. They were unbelievably sweet and
at that perfect point of ripeness, a teetering balance that might
tomorrow fall to the bitter side of spoilage. My frenzy eased.
I started dropping them into the bucket, which at first plunked
as each berry hit the empty bottom but soon was silent as the
ripe harvest accumulated.

There had been rain almost all summer, and the days had been cold. I can't remember ever keeping a fire in the wood-stove in July. But that summer, in the mornings, I had most reluctantly crumpled newspaper, snapped sticks in two, and lit the blaze to warm my summer room. As I stood out at the edge of the great field, the sun warmed my neck and my shoulders like an old friend come home. Crows lofted above in their mysterious flights from limb to limb, hoarsely crying, while crickets sung along. Bright yellow goldenrod nodded in the afternoon breeze. I wanted to stay out there forever, picking through an endless summer's day.

The jug holds two quarts and soon the button-sized berries mounded above the rim. I turned reluctantly back toward the house, thinking how these berries could be used. I thought about making a pie. I thought about making jam, which I always hesitate to do because it takes so many berries to boil down to a pint. But the reward is good, on toast, unbelievably sweet. I thought maybe I would freeze them, and bring them out on a winter night.

When I got back to the kitchen, I put the jug up onto the counter. The phone rang and it was an old friend, wanting to get together. "Come over," I said. "I'll put something on the grill." He came and we sat outside on the grass, eating our meal from chipped plates. We had not seen each other in a long while so our sentences ran into each other's, a flowing stream. The smell of the fresh cut hay was all around us. The big orange sun was getting ready to drop behind the trees.

From down in the hollow, the crows let loose with a great commotion of shrill cackles. We fell silent. They sounded drunk or as if they had struck gold. "I think," I said to my companion, "they found the blackberry patch."

The heat of the day was behind us. We gathered our plates and went inside. "How about some berries?" I offered. There was no resistance. I measured out the jug into big bowls and poured cream into a pitcher. We sat down at the table, in front of the open windows, where we could still hear the jubilation of the crows. The berries were still warm from the sun, sweet like sugar. The dark, wine-like color stained our bowls and our lips. There would be no pie, no jam, no winter berries. These berries were for the moment and no moment could have been more perfect.

✵ *Cable Free*

I SUPPOSE RED FOX FANS are nationally famous — maybe even internationally famous. Perhaps it is my contrary nature or the fact that all my ancestors came from New York but I'm not a Red Sox fan. There. It's been said. I grew up rooting for Mickey Mantle and Roger Maris and, to some degree, this love — and I think that's what it is — has never left me.

But I can't watch their games on television. Up here on the hill, the word "never" is used when we inquire when we might be able to hook into cable. Of course, that leaves us with the option of the "dish" but I'm not a big television fan and I can't justify the expense. I putter along with the weak reception of a small antenna. I'm able to get the three basic networks which offer adequate options. I don't really know why anyone would need more. Except when it comes time for the World Series. In 1986, on a small black and white television (fine-tuned with rabbit ears), I watched Bill Buckner let the hopes of all of New England roll between his legs. But times have changed and those of us without cable are now locked out of this All-American drama.

A couple of years ago, when the Yankees were poised to go up against the Arizona Diamondbacks, I had to find a way to watch the games. I could have gone to a sports bar but that would require a lot of time spent in an unfamiliar environment. That would also require me to sit among a lot of Red Sox fans. Not a pretty thought. I also thought about renting a motel room so that I could watch in private. But by the time the play-offs were over, the price of the room might equal the cost of a dish plus a year of viewing. So, perhaps I could impose on a few friends? Well, if you can imagine trying to find a friend who would endure watching the Yankees do anything but lie down and die at the hands of the Red Sox, then you have a very generous imagination. At last, I remembered friends from Boston who have a summer place here in town — with cable connection. I mustered my courage and called them at their winter home to ask if I could use their summer house to watch the play-offs. Yes, of course, they graciously said, and they sent me a key.

A thrill raced through me. On the night of the first game, I drove over to the dark, deserted house. I let myself in. The house was colder than outdoors. I found a blanket and wrapped it around my shoulders. To my amazement, the Yankees won. The next night, I returned, dressed more warmly. I sat wrapped like a mummy, eyes glued to the tube. The competition teetered one way and then the other, the Diamondbacks inching ahead, then the Yankees triumphing. When Scott

Brosius hit his last minute, game-saving home run in the eleventh inning, I leapt to my feet, threw the blanket off and, in the quiet stillness of my friends' house, I cheered like a lunatic. On the screen, the noise from the fans was deafening. I felt part of something distant, unquantifiable, and thrilling, which I guess is what being a fan is all about.

At last, I silenced the television, snapped off the lights, and went back outside into the cold October midnight. On the way home, I didn't see a single light on, anywhere. I realized as I drove along the darkened roads, I was very likely the only one in town who had watched the Yankees win. Or cared. In another heartbreaking game, my Yankees lost the play-offs to those Arizona upstarts. That news was buried on the last page of the local paper. I believe that, if they could have gotten away with it, the newspaper, deep in Red Sox territory, would have just as soon left it out altogether. But I saw it and I remembered every run.

ॐ *Summer Dance*

WE HAVE A SIZABLE summer population around here. They come from Boston or New York or Florida and places in between, to Dublin and Silver Lake and some of the smaller lakes like Tolman Pond. When I first lived here, I didn't know any of these people and my husband and I disliked the interruption this influx brought. Suddenly, the lakes and ponds were alive with boats and the general stores were crowded with unfamiliar faces. We preferred our year-round life and looked forward to September, when we could once again row the waters in the quiet of the morning mist.

I look back on that time like a portion of childhood, when life has not quite explained itself and certain doors have not yet opened. Many of these summer people are close friends now, an integral part of the deep breath of the summer season. They come, altogether, and, like separated lovers, we rejoice at seeing each other once again. There are gatherings and stories told, and the habits of the summer come back like remembered dance steps. Here we are, together again!

For those of us who are here all year, these summer visitations are woven into the work of the rest of the season. We are not on vacation but working, taking to the desk each morning, to the garden in the afternoons, and balancing all the summer tasks as best we can, through the short, demanding season. But there is this added dimension that carries us just a little further, long walks together, distance swims, or, even better, night swims and all those lazy evenings on the porch, rocking, watching the lake go dark and catching up. I see this influx now not as a hindrance but a gift that they bring us.

September, often being the most beautiful of all our brief summer months, comes quickly and their exit always seems too soon. But these decisions are often made by school calendars rather than love of the season.

Last summer, one of our neighbors who are only here in the summer decided to retire early and stay through the year. My heart soared at the idea of having friends here on the road all year round. I imagined cold winter nights playing Scrabble beside the woodstove, movies together, long walks with the dogs. September came and the great exhale began, as one after another packed up and headed south, to New Jersey, to Pennsylvania, to Florida. The "refrigerator" parties (wherein everyone gets together and shares what is left in their refrigerator before the appliances are unplugged for the winter) all took place amid a warm and forgiving September. Against the template of those early days when Paul and I rejoiced to see all the summer folk go home, I think of this exodus now more like the first frost. The great race of summer is over. The burgeoning plenty of the vegetable garden — so much to give away! — lies dead, tangled in blackened vines, a wasteland made of yesterday's abundance. And so it goes with the summer houses, suddenly shuttered, docks pulled up, boats in the shed, windows dark.

Still, my friends down the road lingered. We gathered for dinner, we went to the movies, we reveled in each other's company and talked about things we could do in the winter. For me, it was as if the garden had escaped the frost. The harvest continued.

But then in October, came the unexpected cold snap — a job offer they couldn't refuse and after an evening of wine and cheese, a few days spent packing up, cleaning out the fridge, and latching shutters, they too were gone, their driveway silent. It was a close call and I thought about it through the winter as snow built up around their house and made entry there impossible. But like the ripeness of summer, they will return, the doors to the old cottage will open, letting in air and light and life and we will start the summer dance, all over again.

ॐ Gathering the Clan

IN THE YEARS SINCE my husband and parents have passed away, I have spent some of the most unusual holidays I could ever have imagined. When I was growing up, on Thanksgiving, the relatives came from all over to gather around one table. Now I often spend the day without any relatives at all. The year that Paul died, I spent Thanksgiving day alone, fasting. And, several years ago, I spent the day on board a sailboat off the coast of Mexico. We had been tossing about on the waves of a storm all night long and I was so seasick that a couple of salty crackers were the limits of the holiday feast. But, more frequently, I have spent Thanksgiving opening my house to friends who have been recently "orphaned," whether through divorce or death or long distances. I do it because I want friends around me and because I know how painful these days can be, when you're alone. No matter how you try to turn your back on the fact, Thanksgiving is a day for families.

One particular Thanksgiving was perhaps the most chaotic of any that I remember. The house here, so recently purchased, had been gutted. A dumpster the size of a boxcar

sat on what once was a lawn. Lumps of plaster and splinters
of lath littered the ground. With a good portion of the house
under construction, I was living in the back part of the el,
which was cold and dreary, piled with boxes of my belongings
that did not yet have a place. Most everything I owned, most
especially my kitchen equipment, was in storage. So I dropped
the idea of doing anything about the upcoming holiday. Let it
go, I told myself. There will be other years.

But, a week before the day, a long-lost cousin called. Pete
was living in Gloucester. It had been years since we had seen
each other. He has been without family for far longer than I.

"What are you doing for Thanksgiving?" I asked.

"Nothing," he said.

"Come here, then."

He came the night before, carrying in from his car boxes
of family photographs and papers. We stayed up late, trying to
reconstruct our family's history. It is a family with a lengthy
past and only a narrow hope for a future. There was a book of
our grandmother's writings, never published but always saved.
We read some of her lines out loud. We peered into the eyes
of our great-grandfather and saw our own. We studied the
sweep of their handwriting and we talked about things that
had happened in our family.

Outside, wind pounded my rattly windows and rain
began. We kept talking, and asking, but there were just the two
of us and most of the answers had died with our parents.

In the morning, I made pancakes while Pete continued to
work through the family papers. In an envelope he found a

folded, yellowing sheet that delineated the path the family took to get to this country from Scotland. At the crown of the tree, the family began, in 1651, when David Sterling settled in Charlestown, Massachusetts. Careful lines of red ink traced his offspring across three pages, taped together to make a spread. The family moved to Lyme, Connecticut, and then to Fairfield. There were marriages that yielded many children with first names like Thaddeus, Rachel, Abigail, and Lockwood. And these names stepped down and down, all the way to the birth of our shared grandmother in Brooklyn, New York. And there the scripted chart ended.

Sheets of water washed down the windows of the old porch. Pete left, mid-afternoon. We hugged and promised to stay in touch. He took the photos but left me with a box full of papers, frail with age. "You can read these, when you have time," he said with a wink. I spent the rest of that day, into the night, reading these papers, and I was deeply grateful that we have always been a family of savers.

I will remember it as one of my richest Thanksgivings, a day that started with just me and Pete and ended with a silent gathering of the clan inside a half-finished house on a hill in a part of New Hampshire where none of them but me had ever lived.

TRANSITIONS

ॐ *The Great Desertion*

MARCH AND APRIL usually mean thaw but last year they meant accumulation. Last winter, during those months, up here on this New Hampshire hill, we received nine feet of snow in the span of forty days. Most of the winter came in the spring. In mid-April, when I usually have peas coming up in my garden, I had mountains of snow surrounding my house, stretching on into the fields. With white everywhere, I felt I would never again see color.

It seemed like the snow and the endless winter were all we had to talk about. Moods rankled. In an effort to cheer us up, roadside signs appeared: Snow for sale, one said. (Ha. Ha.) Another, on a church, was more philosophical, posing the question, When the snow melts, where does the white go? In the next town, a woman advertised that at 7 in the evening on a Friday night, she would be leading a group primal scream, for anyone who was having trouble containing their emotions from behind those high drifts. I wanted to go and scream with the rest of them but could not get out of my driveway. I heard, though, that a lot of people came out of their houses, gathered in a tight circle on the town common, and let forth one gigantic, hell-bent-for-leather scream.

Certainly the winter had not been all bad. There was some great skiing and the snowshoeing, at least in the early part of the winter, was memorable. Neighbors found that sledding from the peak of their barn roof offered a good thrill. Deep snow hid the familiar landmarks of our terrain like a great white coverlet and made certain chores easier. One bright April morning, I pulled the lopping shears off the hook in the garage, strapped on my snowshoes, and walked out across the high white terrain to my cherry tree. The tree was completely buried, with just the top branches sprouting out of the snow. Bending down as if weeding, I cut the branches level with the snow. I felt mighty, standing as I was above the fourteen-foot tree. I marveled at how easily I could reach what, at any other time of the year, would have required a ladder. And balance.

But even the actual first day of spring let us down. A friend of mine and I planned to meet at a Boston area restaurant that's so popular, one must make reservations months in advance. We did so, back in February, with snow to the windowsills, savoring the idea of spring and the great daydream of feeling warm temperatures and seeing bulbs pushing up out of newly thawed earth. Instead, we had to cancel our rendezvous as two more feet of snow landed on us the night of the equinox. With the abundance of snow, Easter seemed like an oxymoron: one of my more dauntless friends organized an Easter egg hunt — on snowshoes. After a while, I felt oddly wedded to the snow and could not imagine life without it.

Our snow left us, all at once, a great desertion. When I drove to New York City on the 18th of April, there was three feet of snow all around my house. The next day the temperatures rose into the nineties, not only in New York but everywhere on the eastern seaboard. The heat stayed. When I returned home to my hill four days later, there was no snow anywhere to be seen. It was gone, as if it had left us in a breath, in a sigh. Like in an Alaskan valley, our grass grew green and the flowers unfolded almost before our eyes. Where, indeed, did the white go. Everywhere I looked, there were pinks and yellows, blues and greens — an abundance of color. Was there any greater, more silent expression of how we really felt about the spring?

ॐ *The Thieving Season*

WHEN THE THAW finally comes, we see the bare ground again for the first time and it always provokes a sharp intake of breath. Like sailors long at sea, we greet the earth with joy. It is brown, the leaves and vegetation from last fall pressed flat from the weight of the snow — actually a dismal scene but, because we know what follows, we take it in on a hopeful note.

When the snow leaves, I go out walking. Snowshoeing and cross country skiing apart, the winter confines us to the roads for our daily walks. But now, stepping off the boat, my dog and I take off into the fields. Mayday runs the way I feel, full speed, in pointless circles. Pure joy. But we are not the only ones who take to the fields when the snow lets go. Around here, we call this time of year the thieving season.

Last year, we went a mile or so, toward a friend's house, which is set back from the road and not lived in during the winter. We watch the house when we can but, in the dark months, the house is walled off from us by the depth of the snows.

When we came up on it, it was sitting proudly on the landscape as it does, and the sight of it was as welcome as the feel of soil beneath our feet. A few branches had fallen from the big oak tree but none had touched the roof. The doors were tight shut, as they had been in the fall, which then seemed so very long ago. I walked around to the back. I saw a shard of glass on the back step and focused on it for a long, startled moment before my eyes traveled up, to the door, which had been pried open. Trails of debris emerged from within the darkness of the shuttered house.

I stepped backward and ran home, where I called the police, who came, in due time, and entered the ravaged house with big flashlights and heavy bootsteps. Eventually, it was discovered that nothing had been taken but everything had been disturbed, trashed, taken apart, and left in pieces on the floor.

I called my friend, the owner of the house who lives in a distant city, and, as if I were reporting a death, I used careful words to tell her what had happened. When the news had been digested, she said, "Don't they know there is nothing there of any value?" meaning, of course, of any value to anyone but her family. "I guess they had to find that out," was all I could say.

She came on the next plane. For several days, in that early season of the year, the traffic on the road increased dramatically as insurance adjusters, police detectives, carpenters, and plumbers began the process of putting her beloved place back to rights.

When they had done their work, I helped her sort through what was left scattered around the floors. We stopped to study the faces of her ancestors before putting the pictures back into the albums. We put tokens from board games back into their boxes and recalled rainy days around the game table. We read the (torn) invitation to her parents' wedding, which had taken place here, in this place of beauty and summer leisure. The damage all around us somehow reminded me of what happens when a bulldozer takes its blade to the contours of a virgin field. It seemed that no matter how well we did our job, the place would never be quite the same again.

It is the sad fact of life in the country that when the ground is open but the summer people have not yet returned, the nasties move about as freely as we do. We can't account for what roams wild out there. In hunting season, we walk cautiously and wear orange to protect ourselves from stray bullets. In thieving season, after our long voyage through winter, we walk swiftly, searching for a hint of green. In the spring, it's somehow harder to remember what lurks. I guess that's this strange thing called hope.

ॐ *To See a Moose*

I T U S E D T O B E the only way to see a moose was to drive way up north, near the Canadian border or into the paper company land in Maine. If a moose was spotted in this area of southwestern New Hampshire, wildlife officials would suppose the animal was "sick." Why else would he (or she) come way down south and show up in people's backyards? They were not always wrong. Some of these animals were sick, especially the one spotted desperately racing around the neighborhoods of Boston last year. But, here, we've gotten used to the fact that we have one more animal to see. And we see them more and more.

Over the past year, I have seen, at different times, a big cow standing in my garden, a pair of what I thought might be young twins drinking at the pond, and a huge buck trotting across the field. From these sightings, I've discovered that moose are wrongly accused of being ugly. Once they set themselves in motion, the rather clumsy looking animal becomes majestic, traversing the terrain with an uncommon grace. It seems you could place a teacup, generously filled, on his back

and, as he gathered speed, the cup and saucer would stay perfectly balanced, as they do in ads for luxury cars.

Once, soon before my mother died, I took her for one last
ride in the car. It was spring, and foliage and creatures were
beginning to emerge. We went to visit a friend who lived near
Dublin Lake. My mother had cancer and her time was drawing near, a fact of which we were all poignantly aware. When
we were about to leave, a call came in that there was a moose
swimming across the lake, an event even rarer than the occasional garden sighting. My mother said, "Oh, I have never seen
a moose!" This quickened my expectations. We hurried into the
car and drove down to the lake to have a look for ourselves.
For no good reason that I can think of now, I thought then
that it would be terrific if my city-bred, seventy-eight-year-old
mother could see a moose before she died. Though her eye-
sight was not strong enough, I was able to spot the moose as
he made his way across the lake, which was newly free of its
ice. I thought that if I could place the car where he would
emerge from the lake, we would be assured of a dramatic sighting, the big animal surging up out of the water. In mere seconds, my mind put together how exciting the scene would be,
how it would thrill my mother.

I drove around to the back side of the lake and parked in
the place where I thought he would come to shore. In the distance, I could see his antlers moving toward us through the
placid water. The configuration of the lakeshore did not quite
allow what I had envisioned. A hedge of bushes would prevent
us from seeing him emerge from the water but, no matter,

he would likely race right by the car, in his fabulously graceful gait.

As he neared shore, he became obscured by vegetation. "He's coming soon!" I said to my mother and she put her hands together in a small muted clap of anticipation. A minute passed and I wondered if I could have calculated wrong. We felt like patrons at the drive-in movie, waiting for the show to start. But, of a sudden, I saw the moose — in my rearview mirror! I had only slightly miscalculated his exit. And, as he disappeared behind us into the deep woods, my mother lost her chance to see a moose. Her last and only chance.

It suddenly seemed so silly, how anxious I had become for her to see something never before seen, indeed, until recently, rarely seen in these parts. We laughed at how greedy we can become to take in all that life has to offer. It seemed we want to pack so much into a life, which, in my mother's case, was a life that had already been quite full, and which, for quite good reasons, had never included the sighting of a moose.

❧ *Ice Damns*

L EST WE GET INTO THE MOOD to celebrate spring
when the month comes round, we are usually
reminded that the great Blizzard of '88 took place in March,
March 18th to be exact. By March of last year, the accumulation of the many winter storms had consolidated into a vast
ice field that stretched as far as my eye could see. For so long,
the snow had been sparkly and deep, but a forceful ice storm
hardened the landscape.

The storms had been awesome and wonderful and I had
enjoyed them all. At one point, the television news in Boston
reported that this had been the "worst winter in thirty years."
I felt a sense of pride sweep over me. Each time a storm was
forecast, I brought out the big drink cooler I use for iced tea
at summer picnics and filled it with tapwater in case I lost
power. If the power goes out here, I'm pretty well set: I can
still cook on my gas and/or woodstove; I have oil lanterns,
fruits, and vegetables in the root cellar; and heat from the
woodstoves as well — but I don't have water as the pump
requires electricity. So I fill the bathtub with water, which

allows me to flush the toilet with a bucket. The cooler of water can last me more than a week. To cater to my other needs, my library of good books serves me well. If it doesn't go on too long, I confess that I look forward to a good outage. It's kind of exciting and cozy and it tests my wits a bit.

Last year at this time, I read Apsley Cherry-Garrard's excruciating record of the ill-fated Scott expedition to the South Pole in 1912. If you are feeling a bit overwhelmed by the ongoing cold of a long winter, this is a great volume to tackle. In it, Cherry-Garrard reports about many extreme discomforts of the season, notably walking through snowstorms in seventy-six below zero, which made my modest reading of twenty-two below zero — recorded from inside my toasty house — seem positively tropical. Later, when the exhausted men are forced to work feverishly with pickaxes to free their ship from the ice, I again felt a sense of companionship with them, slight thread though it was.

As the winter eases out here, there seems to be an ice season not unlike that which closed in on those hapless sailors. Romantic icicles hanging from the roof lines turn into harbingers of the dread ice dams, strange phenomena wherein the heat that escapes through the roof melts the underside of the snowload and drips down, only to freeze into "dams" at the cold, unheated edge of the roof. Thus the continual melting is backed up and has nowhere to go but inside the house. The high winds here at the farm are useful in keeping the snow off the roof which avoids this hazard but I find ice in other places. While many of my friends were on the phone to their insurance agents about their ruined walls or ceilings, I chipped away at the dams that were rising up just about everywhere.

But each warming day gives us hope. On the first day of March of last year, the temperature rose to a balmy forty degrees and I went outside in my t-shirt to work with a pick-axe on the huge mock glacier that had formed at the threshold to the garage, effectively barring entry. I chopped in the pleasing temperatures and thought of Cherry-Garrard and his companions in that long-ago time of adventure and deprivation. The sun was strong and higher in its axis, a great help in removing the ridge that had slowly risen throughout the winter months. It often seems to me that spring here is about the tiny, incremental but nonetheless rewarding steps toward warmth.

৵ *The Beginning of Time*

T O THE EAST OF THIS FARMHOUSE is a pond, not much of a pond but nonetheless, it's there in all seasons. It's small enough so that most people who come here are surprised when I mention "the pond." "What pond?" they ask and I have to take them over to see it, at the edge of the field. There are tall grasses that grow around the edge, too, which contribute to the camouflage. In the fall, the pond is especially inconspicuous, except for the great bush of winterberries that emerges from the edge of the water. The bush is there all summer but it's just greenery, matching the alderbush that surrounds it. But by November, the berries flare red, a brilliant high fan of color that outlasts our falling leaves. The easiest place to see the pond is from my upstairs bedroom window. Perhaps because it is often the first thing I see when I wake up, I use the pond as a touchstone. When the water is low, it looks dark, almost black, but more often, it is white, a reflection of the sky and I think of it as the clear eye of my field, looking back at me.

At its lowest ebb, the pond forms an almost perfect circle and the dark water seems bottomless. When I first bought
this farm, I often wondered about the source of this water. I
had been told that it was a "run-off" pond. There's no doubt
that rainwater contributes to the pond. During a good rain, I
can almost watch the level rise, like an incoming tide. But if it
were just rain that filled it, the pond would vanish in the dry
seasons. Since I've never known it to go dry, the pond seemed
to have more to it than just rainwater. My answer came unexpectedly one day when one of the local firemen stopped by
to ask for a donation to the town fire company. We got talking and he turned his attention to the pond. "You've got a
gusher there," he said. When I asked him what he meant, he
said that they had come up here for a drill once, a few years
back, and filled the tanker from my pond. "We pumped a long
time and we could have kept on. That spring was pumping as
fast as we were!"

That confirmed what I had thought, what I had hoped:
the little pond had a deep source.

In winter, snow shutters the pond. The first freeze glazes
the surface and I think about getting out my skates. But the
snow always comes sooner — and takes away the pond. The
eye closes and I soon forget that it's there.

The spring finds it for me. Spring rains open the field and
bring the pond, pregnant with snowmelt and spring rain, to its
full shape, sprawling out into the field. And the chorus begins:
just one voice at first, a hesitant, cautious *peep . . . peep . . . peep*
— a tuning up. On those first gentle warm nights, I open my

windows and touch the screens, a gesture that reassures me that winter has gone. I hear that one voice, a shy heartbeat coming from the water, newly freed of its ice. If I were to record this symphony and give it a name, I'd call it "The Beginning of Time" as another voice slowly joins the first brave one, and a polite conversation begins. *Peep. Peep peep. Peep peep peep. . . . Peep.* Where do they come from, these tiny frogs-to-be? As the eye of the pond opens to the warmth of the spring air, I picture them swimming up from the depth of that spring, a vein that connects us to that great subterranean lake, the aquifer that laps beneath the field.

The nights increase and we reach the balancing moment of the equinox, a time so poised, so perfectly aligned that some claim they can make eggs stand on end. I don't need to see eggs standing on end to know that the earth has come into a good place. The reeds have begun to grow again and the branches of the winterberry are putting out tiny green shoots. With every new warm day, more peepers join the throng, their voices growing louder, more frequent, until it all sounds like voices in the crowded room of a whole new world, a roiling, noisy debate that calls attention to my secret pond and comforts me all through the nights of April.

ॐ *The First Cut*

M AY IS A DYNAMIC MONTH, with lots of changes and surprises. It is a month of movement, a month of greening grasses and opening leaves. In my own life, May has brought as much pain as happiness. Like some personal oracle, the month marks births and deaths, exciting new projects as well as disappointments, and a little dog I call Mayday. All these events came to me without warning or plan. However, one thing I can count on in May is the resurrection of the lawn.

The lawn here was never planted, or so I assume. I believe it was simply part of the hayfields that extend out on all four sides of this house. Friends who live in more suburban areas sometimes visit and emote about the beauty of my lawn — so deep, so dense, so weed free! I take no credit. I like to keep it cut as it provides that civilized circle of green where I can play croquet with the neighbors or lie on hot nights and observe the sky. This soft apron also provides a buffer zone between the house and the wild where Mayday can rule. If I did not mow it, I believe I could let the grass grow to height and then cut it and bale it, something not possible with grass grown from seeds developed specially for lawns.

But I do love to mow the lawn. For this I have a small green riding mower, shaped like a miniature tractor. This tractor starts with a key, which is worth remarking on because the tractor that preceded it, a Farmall BN, started like an old Model T, with the turn of a crank in front. This starting motion was a practiced maneuver that, if not done right, could result in a thrown shoulder. That never happened to me but I was always aware of that possibility as I jerked the rod with a vigorous motion and heard, with relief, that sweet engine come to purring life. And so, as I settle into the padded seat (another plus) of the little riding mower, I'm always grateful to simply turn the key in the ignition and let the wonders of modern mechanics do the rest.

Last May came early, or so it seemed. The daffodils — some of which Mary planted years ago and some of which I have planted in my few years here — were brought into full bloom by an early heat wave which also forced the forsythia into its egg yolk yellow song. In preparation for that spring cutting ritual, I had had the tractor's blades sharpened, the oil changed, and I'd filled the tank with fresh gas. On the third Friday of the month, the grass was that wonderful brilliant green poets sometimes call emerald but which we simply call spring green. It was high enough to cut and I was more than ready and willing. I went to bed eager to rise early for the task. But as Saturday morning dawned, snow raced, blizzardlike, past the windows and, within a matter of hours, masked the spring that had been building for weeks. When it was all over, several inches covered the grass, and weighted the daffodils and forsythia in cold insult. My Saturday had to be retooled — I put wood in the stove as I had been doing for the past six months, and went to work at my desk. Within a week, the snow was gone and the tractor and I had our delayed reunion, a great circling of the big lawn, which rewarded me with that incomparable scent of the first cut. I had thought the spring had come early but it came late instead. But that was May — above all, a surprise.

ॐ The Winter Mooring

THE FIRST HOUSE I OWNED in this area was in the woods, a small Cape. When the leaves were off the trees, from the upstairs bedroom window I could see the sparkle of the water of Seaver Pond, a part of a chain of lakes that passes through the town. In between the lakes, the streams ebb and flow with the action of the dams. I can only imagine all the factories that ran on the power of this water. I know that one made clothes pins. Another belted out woolens. I have heard that, back then, a thick residue and the brilliant colors of industry accumulated on certain ponds. People living then understood the purpose of the waters that surrounded them but they probably didn't have much chance to enjoy them or worship their beauty. This is our privilege.

When my husband was alive, we used to put our boat into Silver Lake just about every night after work and often we'd go out at sunrise as well. It didn't matter if we didn't have a house on the water. Our boat gave us all the proximity to the lake we could hope for. As long as the water was free of ice, we'd set forth. We'd row past the cottages, smell the bacon cooking, see smoke rising from a chimney, and keep rowing, until there was just open water and trees at the edge. No one else but us. There, we'd swim or drop a line in. We'd let the boat drift. Great blue herons would startle up out of the bog. Loons would cry and, once or twice, surface next to the boat, fixing a red eye on us.

The boat was made by a boatbuilder on Cape Cod for an elderly man who went blind shortly after he took possession of the little craft. We bought the boat from him with a mixture of excitement over our new purchase and sadness for the man who had never been able to use what he so obviously had wanted. I often think of him and all the peaceful evenings he missed out on. The boat is flatbottomed and stable, painted white on the outside and dark gray on the inside, a color scheme we kept like the tenets of a religion.

I still have the boat, but I don't go out in it as often. When I do, the experience is just as magical. On good evenings, I sometimes push off, setting the leathers (which I stitched on myself) into the oarlocks, dropping the oars (so perfectly varnished by Paul) into water so clear you can see twenty feet down to the bottom. The rhythm of the rowing, lift and drop, lift and drop, can soothe just about any anxieties I have ever had.

I think then not only of Paul, who had not rowed much until we married, but also of my uncle, an old salt who taught me to row when I was nine or ten. He was stern and untrusting of my abilities, since I tended to be a difficult and restless child. "Shipshape!" he'd holler at me and I'd squirm into the middle of the seat, balancing the dinghy before setting the oars into the water. And off we'd go, skittering like a waterspider.

It seemed to take years before I found the rhythm I now know without thinking, pulling the two oars like one piece.

I also now think of Ruth Farris, a woman I knew in Cutler, Maine. After her husband died, she rowed every day, as far into winter as she could, which is pretty far since the harbor doesn't freeze the way a lake does. The people of her town expected to see her, most days, pulling her oars across the harbor and back to her cove. She told me it is the most soothing thing she knew of and that whenever she got het up about anything, she would go for a row. Ruth is dead now but she remains a legend in her town and beyond, the action of her oars visible on foggy days.

In the fall, I reluctantly bring my little boat home, imagining a summer when I will, once again, go out every night and early mornings too. It takes two to carry the boat to the barn so I always enlist the help of a friend. Together we lift the upside down pram from the back of the pickup. The oarlocks dangle from their chains as we walk through the wide open doors of the big barn. In the back, where chickens once pecked the dirt floor, a set of sawhorses await. We sidestep into position, eyeballing the proportion of boat to sawhorse until it's balanced just right and we bring her to rest on her wooden winter mooring. I run my hand over the bottom, the paint flaky from a summer of sun and water. I think about the spring, when I'll start to scrape and smooth her, apply the special marine paint and then the spar varnish to her gunwales. It's a special kind of love that paints a good boat and it's a good boat that can take you to so many extraordinary places within the circle of a modest lake and a life so short.

✥ *Fresh Paint*

IN THE FALL OF 2001, I was beset with the feeling that things change all too fast, and sometimes without good reason. Some parts of the landscape near here were starting to look like everywhere else on earth and reverberations of the terrorist attacks in New York could still be felt very strongly. These are both things over which I have no control but which brought a deep sadness to my heart. When I'm sad, I try to get busy, which is never much of a problem here. There are always many things that need doing.

One of the chores I take on in the fall is painting and last fall I tackled the Adirondack chair. The chair once belonged to my grandparents. I have an old snapshot of the two of them sitting in this chair and its mate, which now belongs to my sister.

I consider this the most comfortable chair I own. The back has a slight recline and the seat rises gradually in the front. The arms are capacious and allow for a pad or book to rest there, while I take time to gaze about at the scenery. The chair is a suitable throne for the out-of-doors and it has come with me, from one home to the next, in my movable life. I don't like to paint it, though, especially chairs which, with all the spindles and arms, have quite a lot of surfaces to reach. I always put the task off until the paint is peeling and unsightly.

My father was a great one for keeping things freshly painted. Our house was his canvas and when he ran out of woodwork or doors or window frames, he continued on to the outdoor furniture. I can well remember him crouching next to this chair, the tin bucket of paint in one hand, the brush in the other, rag protruding from the back pocket of his khaki pants. When he painted, he always leaned close to his work and took great pains with the details. Just before finishing a job, he would take the brush and just lightly stroke over the surface, to remove any sign of the brush. Everything he painted had a smooth, enamel finish.

And so, feeling that terrible sense of melancholy rising up, I went out to the barn to paint the Adirondack chair. I always think of my father when I paint. Each step of the way, even the simple opening of the can, moving the screwdriver carefully around the lid, brings his methods to mind. As I went about the task, I thought about the chair and its long legacy. It is made of solid oak and there is only a slight hint of rot at the very bottom of the square legs. I wondered how many times it had been painted, first, I suppose, by my grandfather, who also always kept a bucket of paint handy for touch-ups, and then by my father. In the thirty years I have owned the chair, I have probably painted it seven or eight times, at least.

Apparently we have all agreed that the color was right. When I scrape it, I can see it has never been any color but white.

It took a couple of good, warm sunny October days to complete the job. I worked in the open door of the barn where sun angled in as I worked through the day but which I could close at night, to protect the project from dew or frost. It was a simple task, one that certainly could not right the wrongs of the world. And yet painting the old chair always brings me an odd sense of satisfaction, a sense of connectedness to a time when a good comfortable seat on a lawn with an open sky above was about all one needed in order to feel right about the world.

Stillpoint

OUR SHORT SUMMER ROCKETS BY — the fall, its comet's tail — and then comes December, not quite winter, but beyond the point of working outdoors on the chores that bring color to our faces throughout October and November.

But then there are those days when we feel the idea of winter was all a masquerade. Even in late November, the sun can come on strong at midday and in spite of the naked landscape, it could be summer. It is, or so we like to think, not quite winter. And so the chairs stay on the porch and on those certain days, we sit outside again in t-shirts and sunglasses and feel the lure of summer return. But the early sunset and uncomfortable chill rebuff. What felt like a dream was a dream. We retreat inside, shut the door, and come to terms with our reality.

I leave to the last the lawn furniture and the truck. These small concessions represent a glimmer of hope for an extended season. Even if the storm to end all storms came barreling at us from out of Quebec, I could get everything in and under cover in fifteen minutes or less. So it doesn't seem like much of a risk to let the chairs stay out on the lawn for those nice days and to keep the truck in the driveway for last-minute jobs.

Of all, I keep the tightest grip on the truck, holding it to the very last minute of late fall. A truck that my husband Paul bought brand new, it's old enough now to qualify as an antique, though it does not look special, only old. The red paint has a patina seen only on weathered metal signs and ancient tractors, and the bottom edges of the doors and fenders end in a lace of rust. Last year we pasted the bed of the truck with fiberglass to keep things from falling down through. The seats are upholstered increasingly in duct tape and the radio (and I do mean radio, not stereo) has not played a tune in many years. But, still, it's so useful, hauling manure, bringing large items home from the auctions and trees from the nursery. Without a truck, I'd have to do without all these things, or so it seems to me. But in the winter, without a load, the truck does not have good traction and, parked as it always is in my driveway, it becomes a burdensome obstacle for the fellow who plows my driveway.

And so, along with the porch furniture and the summer clothes, the truck gets mothballed and tucked away for the winter. Usually this happens in December. Keeping an eye on the weather as the season closes, I also keep an eye on the gas gauge. I don't want to store the truck with a full tank of gas so I take the truck on errands and let the level go down, to almost empty. If I have to, I buy just a couple of dollars' worth to keep it going until the day is right. I think of this as the last task, the closing of the door on the outdoor season and it usually takes place in the cold wind of an oncoming storm.

Inside the red barn, I rearrange the chairs and tables stored here and there and make space for their winter companion. In spitting snow, I carefully back the truck into the narrow space — so cramped that once it's in place, I have to crawl out the passenger side door and then climb over the hood to get out the door. I take a good look: the truck, grill facing out, looks ready, even eager, to exit in the spring. I roll the big door shut and set the latch, a sound that is followed by a certain stillness. The truck engine is still. The garden is still. The lawn and the tractor are still. Even the pond, without the ducks and the noisy summertime frogs, is still. In stillness is waiting. Winter has begun.

There are those, I suppose, who find this melancholy. Sad. A long stretch of dark days and long nights, the brightness of summer at the other end of the galaxy. And I think so too. Standing out there in the driveway, my collar pulled up against the cold wind, there's a moment, a breath, during which I feel a sense of sadness for what has passed and dread for what is to come. Oh, the wonderful summer is over! Punishing winter has begun! But then, there is a dawning. The stillness evokes relief, a relief not unlike climbing into a familiar and comfortable bed after a long and hard day, the sense of a job well done coming to a welcome rest — closing one's eyes and floating off into a dream.

The short day is coming to a close by the time I get back inside the house. There, the fire is cracking in the kitchen stove, evoking a cheerful feeling that comes not only from the warmth of the flames but also from knowing that the wood-shed is full of good wood and the bucket is full of dry kin-dling. And night is beginning to fall. It might be that I am exceptional in my love of the nights. During the summer, there is so little time to read the books I want to read. Magazines pile up. I can't bear to throw them away until I've read them. But who can spend time reading when there are gardens to work and mountains to climb? Nights are now for reading and working at the desk in the deep, unbreakable silence of winter.

Soon will be the solstice, that magical night of darkness which, if we're lucky, is accompanied by a big round white moon whose glinting light on fresh snow can make mockery of winter's darkness.

Once the truck is inside the barn, my mind can rest. The work is done. Everything — the garden, the flowering shrubs, the tall maples and oaks, the tractor, the truck, the very barn itself — can rest in the stillpoint of our winter imagination.

ঞ Couch Dreams

IT'S ALWAYS SAID THAT going without can make us appreciate what we may otherwise take for granted and, since moving here, I've found that to be quite true. Central heat was never something I had considered to be a luxury, nor was something so common as a couch. But when we first began the renovations and I moved into the back part of the house, I lived sparely for a longer time than I had originally thought. The accent is on *sparely*. While the new part of the house took shape in the warm, south-facing part of the house, I sat downstairs, in the dark northern el, on a hard wooden kitchen chair or deep in my bed, for those were my only two furniture options.

Somewhere in that first year, I developed what I began to refer to as "couch dreams." First of all, these fantasies involved having a living room, which I did not have. And second of all, they involved having a couch, which I longed for, in the same way that one longs for sun in the middle of an endless snowy winter. I began to think about the couch as if it were a physical place where I could go, like the beach on a Caribbean island or a sailboat gently rocking at anchor. Every once in a while, sitting at my desk, my mind would drift off to this fantastic place: I would be reclining on a luxuriant sofa, reading a great novel. The sun would be streaming in the windows and the warmth would put me to sleep, in that delicious way when all cares are taken from us and we are completely at ease.

In spite of my dreams, the renovations went at their own pace. After a year's work, the kitchen emerged, a wonderful sunny room with warming stoves, spacious counters, and floors painted the color of ballpark mustard. This was great progress. But the hard kitchen chairs followed me when I moved into that space. Still couchless, I continued the fantasies.

In the fall, Michael and Henri, the steadfast carpenters who had guided me throughout the difficult birthing of this new home, cut through the kitchen wall to begin work on the new living room. They labored for some time on that room, a small space, made smaller by their tools and machinery. When they had wedged the last of the beech floorboards into place, swept up the wood shavings, and packed up their tools, the room sat still and quiet, an empty space alive with possibilities.

The time had come to buy a couch. On a rainy Saturday, I set forth. I took a friend, Rosemary, a woman who understands all that a comfortable perch can mean. Together we mapped out a route and began the journey, from one furniture gallery to the next. Efficient, focused, we entered each store and made our way through the displays, quickly eliminating the frilly, the incredibly overstuffed, the outrageously priced, and the sofas sized appropriately for an auditorium. When we found one that engaged us, we sat down and stayed awhile. Was it too hard? Could it double as a bed, if need be? Did it allow us to get back on our feet without a struggle?

By the end of the day, we had a list of possibles, along with measurements. I returned to the empty room and did some sizing. After that, the list was down to two. Alone, I drove back to the competing stores and studied the contenders. One of the first we had chosen had stayed with me throughout the search. It had rounded arms and stubby feet, and the edges were studded with big upholstery hobnails. The fabric was olive, with dark red and black threads woven in. It looked like a couch made in the 1930s. Soft, a bit dowdy, and very welcoming.

One chilly Sunday afternoon, not too long after my new acquisition had been delivered, I lit a fire in the new room. Armed with a good book, I settled on the couch. The warmth from the hearth spread throughout the room, adding to the heat already spawned by the sun. Somewhere perhaps into the second chapter, I stretched out and continued to read. I remember, as I began to doze, thinking about all those cold days, reading upright in the hard chair. I remembered because I was about to live my dreams. When I woke up, the book was on the floor beside me, the sun on my face, the logs down to rosy embers.

PHOTO BY ANN CARD

EDIE CLARK has been a writer and editor of books and magazines for the past 30 years. She has written extensively about New England in award-winning feature stories for *Yankee* magazine, where she served variously as Senior Editor, Senior Writer and Fiction Editor for nearly 25 years. Her memoir, *The Place He Made,* was described by the *New York Times Book Review* as "a triumph of the human spirit (which) may take its quiet place among the best of the literature." She wrote the text to *Monadnock Tales,* a fusion of music and poetry which has been performed several times in the Monadnock Region of New Hampshire. She has been a fellow at the MacDowell Colony and also at Hedgebrook, on Whidbey Island, Washington. She is currently Contributing Editor to *Yankee* magazine. She teaches writing in workshops and writing programs and gives frequent talks throughout New England. To learn more about her work, visit www.edieclark.com.

Order Form

To order more copies of this book, go to www.edieclark.com or use this order form:

NAME: _____

MAILING ADDRESS: _____

_____

CITY & STATE: _____

TELEPHONE: _____

E-MAIL: _____

Please send _____ copies of *The View from Mary's Farm* at $14.95 per copy plus $4 for shipping and handling.

Send order form and check or money order to:

Mary's Farm
P.O. Box 112
Dublin NH 03444

For information on bulk orders and publisher's discounts, go to **www.edieclark.com.**